WRITERS AND THEIR WORK

General Editor
ISOBEL ARMSTRONG

Advisory Editor
BRYAN LOUGHREY

The Sensation Novel

'DREAMING LOVE AND WAKING DUTY'
by ROBERT BARNES ARWS 1840–1895 from *London Society* 1862, vol. 2

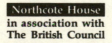

The
Sensation
Novel

from *The Woman in White* to *The Moonstone*

Lyn Pykett

Northcote House
in association with
The British Council

© Copyright 1994 by Lyn Pykett

First published in 1994 by Northcote House Publishers Ltd, Plymbridge House,
Estover Road, Plymouth PL6 7PZ, United Kingdom.
Tel: (0752) 735251. Fax: (0752) 695699.

British Library Cataloguing-in-Publication Data
A catalogue record for this book is available from the British Library

ISBN 0 7463 0725 X

Typeset by Kestrel Data, Exeter
Printed and bound in the United Kingdom by BPC Wheatons Ltd, Exeter

Contents

Abbreviations and References

Wherever possible I have taken quotations from the novels of the 1860s from widely available paperback editions. Details are given in the Select Bibliography.

A	*Armadale,* by W. Collins (Oxford, 1980)
AF	*Aurora Floyd,* by M. E. Braddon (Oxford, 1987)
CUF	*Cometh Up as a Flower,* by R. Broughton (London, 1898)
EL	*East Lynne,* by E. Wood (London, 1984)
JML	*John Marchmont's Legacy,* by M. E. Braddon (London, 1863)
LAS	*Lady Audley's Secret,* by M. E. Braddon (Oxford, 1987)
M	*The Moonstone,* by W. Collins (Harmondsworth, 1986)
NN	*No Name,* by W. Collins (Oxford, 1986)
WW	*The Woman in White,* by W. Collins (Oxford, 1980)

1

The Sensation
Phenomenon

WHAT WAS SENSATIONAL ABOUT THE SENSATION NOVEL?

> That bitter term of reproach, 'sensation,' had not yet been invented for
> the terror of romancers in the fifty-second year of this present century;
> but the thing existed nevertheless in divers forms, and people wrote
> sensation novels as unconsciously as Monsieur Jourdain talked prose.
>
> (M. E. Braddon, *The Doctor's Wife*, vol. 1, pp. 10–11)

In 1863, in the pages of the *Quarterly Review* (a heavyweight organ
of conservative opinion) Henry Mansel, Dean of St Paul's, launched
a fierce critical and moral attack on a species of fiction which was
just then enjoying considerable success. The literary phenomenon
about which Mansel wrote – in both sorrow and anger – was the
sensation novel, which, he claimed: 'must be recognised as a great
fact in the literature of the day, and a fact whose significance is by
no means of an agreeable kind'.[1] Nearly one hundred and twenty
years later Patrick Brantlinger described the sensation novel as 'a
minor subgenre of British fiction that flourished in the 1860s only to
die out a decade or two later'.[2]

A 'great fact' in the literature of its day? A 'disagreeable' sign of
its times? An ephemeral, minor subgenre? What was the sensation
novel? Why did it come to dominate the literary scene for a time in
the 1860s? What did it signify? What, if anything, does it have to
offer to late-twentieth-century readers of novels, students of fiction
and students of Victorian culture? These are some of the questions
which this study will try to address.

The 1860s was the sensation decade; a decade of sensational events
and sensational writing. It was the age of ' "sensational" advertise-
ments, products, journals, crimes, and scandals';[3] the age of sensational 'poetry, art, auction sales, sport, popular science, diplomacy

1

and preaching'.[4] The 1860s was also, pre-eminently, the age of the sensational theatre, most notably the stylized dramatic tableaux, heightened emotions and extraordinary incidents of melodrama. As Michael Booth has so amply demonstrated, in *Victorian Spectacular Theatre, 1850–1910* (1981), this was an age of increasingly spectacular 'special effects', involving dioramas, panoramas, elaborate lighting systems and machinery of all kinds. Theatrical illusion and the Victorian machine culture combined in a new technology of representation. In short, this decade was a moment of consolidation in the 'era of the spectacle' – inaugurated by the French Revolution, and consolidated by the Great Exhibition of 1851 and the International Exhibition of 1862 – in which the 'mode of amplification and excess' became 'a mode of producing the *material* world'.[5]

Private affairs were turned into public spectacle in the theatre of the courtroom. A novel form of real life drama drew the salaciously inclined to the newly constituted divorce courts (following the Matrimonial Causes Act of 1857) to hear details of marital deception, discord and misalliance. The colourful Yelverton bigamy–divorce case (a long-running legal wrangle which started in 1857) attracted a great deal of attention in 1861. It highlighted the chaotic state of the marriage laws and marriage customs, and provided the sensation novelists with many incidents for their plots.

The criminal courts also threw the spotlight on to 'the secret theatre of home'[6] with a plethora of sensational trials for crimes of passion and tales of domestic violence. Murderous women were especially in the news, most notoriously Madeline Smith, who poisoned her lover by putting arsenic in his cocoa (1857), and Constance Kent the sweet 16-year-old who was accused of stabbing her 4-year-old brother in 1860. The details of all of these cases of bigamy, divorce and murder were communicated to the ever-widening readership of a rapidly expanding newspaper press by the sensational reporting then enjoying a vogue. Sensational journalism (like sensation fiction) was seen by many as a form of creeping contagion, the means by which the world of the common streets, and the violent or subversive deeds of criminals were carried across the domestic threshold to violate the sanctuary of home.

The sensation novel was among the chief sensations of this sensational decade. According to contemporary commentators on the literary scene the sensation novel was a mushroom growth, a new kind of fiction which appeared from nowhere to satisfy the cravings

2

of an eager and expanding reading public possessed of suspect, or downright depraved tastes. 'Two or three years ago', observed a writer in the *Edinburgh Review* in 1864:

> nobody would have known what was meant by a sensation novel; yet now the term has already passed through the stage of jocular use . . . [and is] adopted as the regular commercial name for a particular product of industry for which there is just now a brisk demand.[7]

In one of many of the examples of 'jocular use' found in *Punch* – a parodic prospectus for an invented journal called *The Sensation Times* – the sensation 'product' was described as:

> devoted to Harrowing the Mind, making the Flesh Creep . . . Giving Shocks to the Nervous System, Destroying Conventional Moralities, and generally Unfitting the Public for the Prosaic Avocations of Life'.[8]

Throughout the 1860s and into the 1870s 'sensation' or 'sensational' were ubiquitous critical or descriptive terms. During this period, as Philip Edwards has noted, 'almost every novel reviewed was either sensational, or remarkable for not being so'.[9] Wilkie Collins, Mary Elizabeth Braddon, Ellen (Mrs Henry) Wood and Rhoda Broughton were indisputably sensation authors (although the extremely long careers of the women took them well beyond the sensation decade and into different fictional territory). Sheridan Le Fanu and 'Ouida' (Marie Louise de la Ramée) were often, perhaps misguidedly, treated as sensationalists. Le Fanu himself rejected the label, claiming (in his Preface to *Uncle Silas*) to belong to the 'legitimate school of tragic English romance'. Ouida's exotic novels of racy high life might also more properly be placed in the romance tradition. Charles Reade used sensation techniques, particularly those borrowed from the domestic melodrama of the theatre (for which he also wrote), but his novels remain essentially 'novels with a social purpose'. Charles Dickens, whose *Great Expectations* was reviewed alongside Collins's *The Woman in White*, undoubtedly shared many of the sensationalists' subjects and methods, and was sometimes included among their numbers. Trollope and George Eliot escaped the label, but, as I shall show in a later section, did not escape the thing. Thomas Hardy made a notable late contribution to the genre with *Desperate Remedies* (published in 1871 but written in 1869) which he dismissed, rather too lightly I think, as a 'highly conventional and sensational tale'. I shall follow Kathleen Tillotson and Philip Edwards in regarding

Collins, Braddon and Wood as the main exponents of the genre, and I shall concentrate on their work.

Variously described as 'fast novels', 'crime novels', 'bigamy novels' or 'adultery novels', sensation novels were pre-eminently tales of modern life. As a reviewer in the *Quarterly* put it:

> The sensation novel, be it mere trash or something worse, is usually a tale of our own times. Proximity is, indeed, one great element of sensation. It is necessary to be near a mine to be blown up by its explosion; and a tale which aims at electrifying the nerves of the reader is never thoroughly effective unless the scene be laid in our own days and among the people we are in the habit of meeting.[10]

These electrifying novels of 'our own days' were mainly distinguished by their devious, dangerous and, in some cases, deranged heroes and (more especially) heroines, and their complicated plots of horror, mystery, suspense and secrecy. The sensation plot usually consisted of varying proportions and combinations of duplicity, deception, disguise, the persecution and/or seduction of a young woman, intrigue, jealousy, and adultery. The sensation novel drew on a range of crimes, from illegal incarceration (usually of a young woman), fraud, forgery (often of a will), blackmail and bigamy, to murder or attempted murder. Formally sensation fiction was less a genre than a generic hybrid. The typical sensation novel was a catholic mixture of modes and forms, combining realism and melodrama, the journalistic and the fantastic, the domestic and the romantic or exotic. Like stage melodrama, with which it had so much in common, the sensation novel was, as Dickens wrote of Wilkie Collins's *The Moonstone*, 'wild yet domestic'.[11]

What were the common characteristics of the narrative structures in which these melodramatic plots were articulated? Thomas Hardy named four key aspects of the sensation narrative in his description of his own attempt at the genre (*Desperate Remedies*): 'Mystery, entanglement, surprise and moral obliquity'. Entanglement and surprise are, of course, commonly found in the heavily plotted Victorian novel, but the sensation narrative is more than usually reliant on surprising events and extraordinary coincidences for its effects, and character is quite often subordinated to incident and plot. Mystery too is a staple ingredient of the mainstream Victorian novel, but in the sensation novel it is the dominant element. The sensation novel, like the detective novel, is the quintessential novel-with-a-secret. The moral obliquity noted by Hardy is just one of the consequences of the sensation narrative's obsession with secrecy. The narrative satisfactions of the sensation novel depend to a great extent on the gradual uncovering of the central secret(s). To this end the most effective sensation writers developed techniques of narrative concealment and delay or deferral. Collins, for example, developed the split or shared narrative which used a variety of first-person narrators, none of whom was in possession of the whole story. Braddon and Wood have recourse to a kind of narratorial coyness, declining (sometimes explicitly, at others implicitly) to disclose crucial items of information, or having key events occur off-stage (so to speak) and only revealing their occurrence at the denouement. The sensationalists in general, and Collins and Braddon in particular, developed a dramatic narrative method, and made a great deal of use of set-piece scenes and dramatic tableaux. Whatever the technique adopted the result was the same: a modification, in some cases quite radical, of the omniscient narrator's role as the reader's guide, guardian and friend. Without this helping hand, and in the absence of all the facts of the case, the reader is left to make provisional moral judgements as the narrative unfolds. The result is a considerable degree of moral ambiguity.

These thrilling novels caused a sensation with both readers and reviewers. The founding texts of the sensation genre – Wilkie Collins's *The Woman in White*, Mary Elizabeth Braddon's *Lady Audley's Secret*, and Mrs Henry Wood's *East Lynne* – were numbered among the best selling novels of the entire nineteenth century. The sensation novel's spectacular success with readers, and the apparent tendency for sensation topics and techniques to invade all areas of contemporary fiction, made the sensation fiction phenomenon one of the hot topics of discussion for the Victorian 'chattering classes'. Many commentators on contemporary life and letters saw the genre as both cause and symptom of the depravity of contemporary morality and the modern sensibility. The existence of the genre was taken to be evidence of a cultural disease, and its success was described as an endemic comparable with the 'Dancing Mania and Lycanthropy of the Middle Ages'.[12] The sensation novel was held to be yet further evidence of that emotional and spiritual degeneracy of modern urban-industrial culture against which Wordsworth had fulminated in his Preface to *Lyrical Ballads* in 1800, when he noted that:

a multitude of causes, unknown to former times, are now acting with a combined force to blunt the discriminating powers of the mind, and . . . reduce it to a state of almost savage torpor. Chief among this multitude of causes, was, the increasing accumulation of men in cities, where the uniformity of their occupations produces a craving for extraordinary incident, which the rapid communication of intelligence hourly gratifies.

The dreadful effects of this situation were, in Wordsworth's view, most clearly evident in the 'literature and theatrical exhibitions of the country', where 'frantic novels' and 'sickly and stupid German tragedies' prevailed in place of the works of Shakespeare and Milton. In the 1860s Wordsworth's condemnation of the modern 'craving for extraordinary incident' was echoed by Henry Mansel, who consigned the sensation genre to 'the morbid phenomenon of literature – indications of a wide-spread corruption, of which they are in part both the effect and cause'.[13] Like many critics of sensation fiction Mansel wrote disapprovingly of its appeal to the reader's animal instincts and physical appetites, and its penchant for 'preaching to the nerves'.

One of the most shocking and thrilling aspects of sensation fiction, as far as its first readers and reviewers were concerned, was the fact that the action of these fast novels of crime and passion usually occurred in the otherwise prosaic, everyday, domestic setting of a modern middle-class or aristocratic English household. In fact both modernity and domesticity are more than simply the *mis-en-scène* of the sensation novel, they are also among its main preoccupations; they become topics of discussion and investigation. In the sensation novel the matter and manner of the gothic tale, the crime novel and domestic fiction meet and mingle in a modern English setting in which 'the England of today's newspapers crops up at every step'.[14] Sensation novels, as Henry James wrote in a much-quoted review of M. E. Braddon's *Aurora Floyd*, dealt with:

> those most mysterious of mysteries, the mysteries which are at our own doors . . . Instead of the terrors of Udolpho, we [are] treated to the terrors of the cheerful country house, or the London lodgings. And there is no doubt that these were infinitely the more terrible.[15]

Another notably shocking feature of the genre was the way in which it represented women and the feminine. Female characters are absolutely central to virtually all sensation novels. Indeed, I shall suggest that one of the genre's most distinctive features was the way in which it displayed women and made a spectacle of femininity, whether of the passive, angelic variety, or in the form of the *femme fatale*. Whether she is the heroine or the villainess (and sometimes the distinction between these two roles is fascinatingly blurred), at least one of the female protagonists in a sensation novel is likely to be assertive, transgressive and a creature of passion, in other words bad, mad, or otherwise dangerous to know. It is worth noting, however, that both nineteenth-century reviewers and twentieth-century re-readers have tended to overestimate the *outspokenness* of sensation heroines, some of whom are remarkable for the power of a feeling which they are *unable to articulate*.

Contemporary reviewers were most scandalized by the sensation text's representation of the sensations of female passion. Margaret Oliphant, in one of several articles on the genre in *Blackwood's*, protested that:

> What is held up to us as the story of the feminine soul as it really exists underneath its conventional coverings, is a very fleshly and unlovely record.

Since the advent of sensationalism, she argued, the heroines of English fiction have been:

> Women driven wild with love for the man who leads them into desperation . . . Women who marry their grooms in fits of sensual passion . . . who pray their lovers to carry them off from husbands and homes they hate . . . who give and receive burning kisses and frantic embraces, and live in a voluptuous dream . . . the dreaming maiden waits. She waits now for flesh and muscles, for strong arms that seize her, and warm breath that thrills her through, and a host of other physical attractions . . . [W]ere the sketch made from the man's point of view, its openness would at least be less repulsive. The peculiarity of it in England is . . . that this intense appreciation of flesh and blood, this eagerness of physical sensation, is represented as the natural sentiment of English girls, and is offered to them not only as the portrait of their own state of mind, but as their amusement and mental food.[16]

Oliphant's outraged femininity in the above extract, particularly in the latter part, also gives us a clue to another important element in the sensation novel's capacity to ruffle the feathers of respectable Victorian society: that is, the central part played by women in the production and mediation of the genre as both writers and readers.

THE CULTURAL MEANING OF THE SENSATION GENRE

> Genre is a socio-historical as well as a formal entity. Transformations in genre must be considered in relation to social changes.[17]

The title of this section, like the title of this study, names a category of fiction whose distinctive features I have attempted (sketchily) to delineate in my opening section. This act of naming and defining a genre involves an attempt to fix something which might more usefully be seen as flexible and changing, as a process rather than an object. Fredric Jameson and Tzvetan Todorov (quoted at the head of this section) have both argued persuasively that genre is a social practice as well as a literary category, a 'socio-symbolic message'[18] which should be seen as a flexible and historically changing set of codes rather than as a fixed formula. My own approach will follow Jameson by attempting to offer a historicized reading of the sensation novel as a process, a socio-symbolic message. However, ironically, as a first step towards understanding the cultural significance of this genre I must note that it was precisely the (perceived) fixed and formulaic quality of sensation novels upon which the critical debate generated by the new genre tended to focus.

> Each game is played with the same pieces differing only in the moves. We watch them advancing through the intricacies of the plot, as we trace the course of an x or a y through the combinations of an algebraic equation.[19]

The formulaic, mechanical nature of the style, structure and content of the sensation novel was generally attributed to contemporary developments in literary production, distribution and mediation. Many (perhaps most) early commentators on the genre focused on it as a commodity in an increasingly commercialized literary marketplace, which was debauched by the 'violent stimulant of serial publication' in periodicals.[20] An increase in literacy and to some extent a growth in the leisuretime in which to read led to a proliferation of tales of 'the marketable stamp'[21] which appeared first in periodicals and subsequently in the volumes issued through the circulating libraries. The spread of railway travel was another significant factor in developing the market conditions for sensation fiction. The sensation novel was, on the face of it, the ideal product for the railway bookstall, offering 'something hot and strong' to entice the 'hurried passenger' and relieve the dullness of the journey.[22] Mass-produced for mass consumption, the sensation novel was used by some critics to mark the boundary between high art and the popular artefact. Unlike the productions of high culture, it was argued, sensation novels were not written to 'satisfy the unconquerable yearnings of the [artist's] soul', rather they were produced by the 'market law of supply and demand' and were 'redolent of the manufactory or the shop'.[23]

Notwithstanding the contemporary insistence on the sterility of the predictable, formulaic nature of the sensation novel, it seems clear (at least with hindsight) that the sensation novel's power to disturb derived substantially from its adventurous and opportunistic mixing of formulas, and its blurring and crossing of generic, stylistic and other boundaries. The sensation novel's roots lie in a wide range of popular forms such as penny magazines, street literature and stage melodrama, as has been well documented by Winifred Hughes and Beth Kalikoff.[24] Indeed, much of the energy and excitement of the sensation novel comes from the way it commandeered and reworked the subject matter and conventions of popular lower-class genres which had grown up alongside the dominant forms of middle-class fiction, but independent of the constraints of middle-class moral management. Written by middle-class authors, addressed (in the main) to middle-class readers and published in middle-class journals, the sensation novel nevertheless cut across class boundaries and, much to the dismay of contemporary reviewers, it temporarily succeeded in 'making the literature of the kitchen the favourite reading of the Drawing room'.[25] Other commentators were more worried about traffic in the other direction, and feared that the pernicious nonsense of sensationalism was passing from the parlour to the kitchen and turning the working classes into revolutionaries. In short, sensation fiction disturbingly blurred the boundaries between the classes, between high art, low art and no art (newspapers), between the public and the private, and between the respectable and the low life or demi-monde.

Sensation fiction was thus both the product and symptom of quite profound changes in fiction and the fiction market in the mid-Victorian period. The sensation debate and the sensation novel itself were also the focus for a range of interrelated social tensions and anxieties. The plots and central preoccupations of sensation novels both embodied and, to some extent, explored the hopes and fears of the Victorian middle classes. They were generated by a range of interconnected anxieties arising from contemporary social changes and the attendant challenging and questioning of the social and moral *status quo*. The chief of these anxieties concerned the nature and status of the family, generally considered to be the cornerstone of Victorian society, perhaps even of civilization itself. Sensation novels are almost always stories of a or even *the* family, and their plots habitually reveal and exploit the fear that the respectable Victorian family had some dark secret at its core.

In addition to this primal fear about the nature of the family, sensation fiction also articulates a range of anxieties arising from changes (or threatened changes) to the organization of the family. Gender roles are central here, and uncertainties about gender roles within the family, the differing expectations about marriage held by men and women, and misunderstandings between marital partners are a recurring theme. The issue of women's role within the family and beyond its boundaries was of particular importance. The Woman Question and the question of woman are perhaps the central preoccupation of this genre, as I have argued elsewhere.[26] Sensation novels reproduce and negotiate broader cultural anxieties about the nature and status of respectable femininity and the domestic ideal at a time when women and other reformers were clamouring for a widening of women's legal rights and educational and employment opportunities. Both implicitly and explicitly these novels raise questions about gender identity, and they both work with and rework prevailing gender stereotypes, such as the 'fast woman' the 'Girl of the Period', the 'Angel in the House', the 'manly man' and the feminized male who lacks a clear social role. Another area of anxiety about the family is manifested in the sensation novel's preoccupation with matters legal, and, in particular, with the role of the law in organizing and controlling the family. This is evident in the sensation novel's obsession with complex legal plots to do with wills and the inheritance of property, with the laws of bigamy and divorce, and with issues arising from women's lack of legal identity and rights (for example, the inability of married women to own property, and the inequitable nature of the divorce and child custody laws).

Finally, two other preoccupations are worthy of note. Both are complexly intertwined with all the other issues and anxieties I have mentioned. The first is social class. Questions of class and the relations between the classes, and a 'social paranoia about infiltration'[27] at a time of great social mobility figured prominently in the sensation novel, as did anxieties about the sustainability of prevailing social and moral codes (the issue of propriety). The other pre-occupation is property, portable and otherwise. Financial insecurity, fears about the chimerical nature of Victorian speculative capitalism, and fears that the solid material comforts of well-to-do middle-class life might have all too insubstantial a base are played out in numerous plots concerning fraud and bankruptcy.

The sensation narrative is perhaps best described by Charles Reade's term, a 'Matter-of-Fact Romance', since, like Dickens's *Bleak House*, it dwells 'on the romantic side of familiar things'. In its mixing of the mundane and the marvellous, the ordinary and the fantastic it becomes the characteristic form for articulating the irrational and/or supra-rational in a materialistic, secular age. In this last respect, as in so many others, the sensation narrative demonstrates its affiliations with melodrama, one of the dominant cultural codes of the nineteenth century. Indeed, we shall gain considerable insight into the cultural meaning and significance of the sensation narrative and the sensation genre if we view it as a particular manifestation of 'the melodramatic imagination'.[28] As Peter Brooks has argued, melodrama is particularly prominent in periods of rapid social change and ideological crisis. In such periods it can perform different kinds of ideological work, functioning either as subversive critique or escapist entertainment. In nineteenth-century Britain, as Martha Vicinus[29] has noted, melodrama served as a 'cultural touchstone' for those classes or social groupings adrift on the sea of social change, and confused or ambivalent about their new role in the emerging social order, and as a 'psychological touchstone' for those who felt themselves to be 'helpless and unfriended', such as the poor and the powerless.

The sensation novel shares the stage melodrama's 'strong emotionalism; moral polarization and schematicization; extreme states of being, situations, action; overt villainy, persecution of the good, and final reward of virtue; inflated and extravagant expression; dark plottings, suspense, breathtaking peripety'.[30] Like the stage melodrama, the sensation novel also tends to displace social and political anxieties into emotional dramas focused on the family. However, whereas in the domestic melodrama of the popular stage an idealized family was represented as the only sure refuge from threatening social upheavals, in the family romance of the sensation narrative

11

the family is merely an illusory sanctuary, and is all too often the source of threatening upheaval.

The sensation novel has been regarded, almost from the moment of its inception, as a minor, marginal and short-lived form. Sensation novels, observed Henry Mansel, had a butterfly existence:

> Written to meet an ephemeral demand, aspiring only to an ephemeral existence . . . they . . . have recourse to rapid and ephemeral methods of awakening the interest of their readers, striving to act as the dram or the dose, rather than as the solid food.[31]

On the whole, literary history has tended to confirm Mansel's judgement. Until relatively recently most sensation novels had disappeared from critical view. This was particularly true of the women's sensation novel, perhaps unsurprisingly given the greater propensity for popular texts by women writers to sink without trace within a generation of their first appearance. Of the writers whose work I shall explore in this study, Collins has continued to be in demand with readers, and has been afforded a place in an expanded canon of English Literature as the father of the modern detective narrative. *East Lynne*, and *Lady Audley's Secret* have persisted in the form of stage melodramas which have remained a fairly constant part of the repertoire of the English theatre, and both have been revived in the early 1990s. For the most part, the sensation genre has been regarded as a historical curiosity, a mere episode in the fluctuating history of public taste, a genre so much the product of its particular historical moment that it was unable to survive that moment.

Sensation novels and sensation fiction have been among the many texts and genres which have been re-viewed in that process of reconfiguring the map of writing which has resulted from both the empirical research and the theoretical developments of the last twenty years or so. The work of reassessing sensation fiction was begun by Kathleen Tillotson and P. D. Edwards (in the essays to which I have already referred), who performed a very useful service in restoring particular sensation novels to critical view, and providing well-informed accounts of the nature and significance of an important literary phenomenon of the mid-nineteenth century. This work was continued in Winifred Hughes's investigation of the sensation genre in relation to mid-Victorian critical debates and literary practices. Hughes's study, published in 1980, gives considerable prominence to the women writers of sensation fiction, following Elaine Showalter's reassessment of them in 1978 (see Bibliography). These feminist re-readings of the sensation genre also provide a context for Jenny Taylor's perceptive reading of Wilkie Collins's use of the sensation narrative to negotiate the contradictions of contemporary discourses about consciousness, identity, and the social formation of the self.

Sensation fiction is also one of a number of cultural fields which has been recovered and reassessed by a newly constituted inter-disciplinary field of cultural studies which has rethought the relations between text and context, reflection and mediation, and production and reproduction. Feminist studies and cultural studies have together profoundly changed our view of what is marginal and what is central, what is 'major' and what is 'minor', and, indeed, of the usefulness of these terms. They have also led to a radical rethinking of the relationship of (or boundaries between) high and low (popular) culture.

Sensation novels still offer an 'exciting read', although some of their 'thrilling' devices, their stereotypical characters and situations, and their rhetorical mannerisms may cause the sophisticated late-twentieth-century reader to smile. Sensation novels also provide interesting reading. I hope that this general introduction has suggested (and that following sections will demonstrate) that sensation novels are of great interest to the student of narrative form. They are also of great interest to anyone who wishes to explore the processes involved in demarcating the boundaries between high art and popular forms, and in the processes by which the components of a living culture are sifted and stratified into a hierarchy of value and become (or fail to become) part of what Raymond Williams has described as the 'selective tradition'.[32] These novels also offer an interesting way of 'reading' mid-Victorian culture, since they were often very direct (and sometimes quite self-conscious) interventions in contemporary social debates. Sensation novels both were produced by and reproduced mid-century anxieties on a wide range of issues. When we look in more detail at the work of the sensation authors we shall see that even when its final inclination was to uphold conventional morality, the sensation novel also probed and questioned Victorian moral and social orthodoxies.

13

2

Wilkie Collins: Questions of Identity

We live . . . in an age eminently favourable to the growth of all roguery which is careful enough to keep up appearances. (*Armadale*, 657)

Of all the sensation novelists, Collins was held in greatest critical esteem by contemporary reviewers. Recent critical reassessments of his work have tended to confirm this placing, and to endorse Collins's own claims to originality as a writer who 'oversteps, in more than one direction, the narrow limits within which [critics] are disposed to restrict the development of modern fiction' (Preface to *Armadale*). Certainly, Collins's self justificatory Prefaces to his novels suggest that he regarded his own fictional practice more seriously than many of his fellow sensationalists – whether as source of shocks and thrills, as social or moral critique, as metaphysical investigation, or as narrative form. Collins was the master of all of the main elements of the sensation genre: the construction and unravelling of an intricate, crossword puzzle plot, the atmospheric scene, the mysterious, prophetic dream, obsessive and disordered mental states, overtly respectable villains, and bold, assertive and/or devious and scheming heroines and villainesses. Moreover, his fragmented, multi-vocal narratives were the boldest experimentations with narrative form to be found in the sensation mode.

The sensational success of Wilkie Collins's *The Woman in White* inaugurated the sensation decade. *The Woman in White* is, for many critics, the 'archetype of the genre' of sensation fiction,[1] and its author is the master of its characteristic form – the novel with a secret. Secretiveness is not only the structuring principle of the sensation plot, it is also its origin, and its subject. Collins's plots (like most sensation narratives) relied heavily upon the combination of roguery, hypocrisy and concealment that, as the quotation from *Armadale* at the head of this chapter suggests, was at the centre of modern life.

14

It has long been argued that Collins's narratives self-consciously unmasked the venality, deception, self-deception and self-seeking that lurked below the surface of Victorian propriety, and offered a critique of Victorian social and moral orthodoxies. More recently, there has been a significant shift of critical attention. Historicized readings of Collins's novels that are also informed by psychoanalytic, semiotic and feminist theories have concentrated on the ways in which his sensation narratives articulate, explore and interrogate the social and psychological processes by which those orthodoxies were constructed and maintained. Viewed from these perspectives Collins's sensation novels are seen to focus on the ways in which individual identities are formed within specific cultural codes, most notably those relating to class and gender, and within particular social institutions such as marriage and the family. They are also centrally concerned with the intervention of the law in each of these areas. The following sections will focus on these issues, and on Collins's preoccupation with problems of subjectivity and perception and with the instability of (modern) identity.

THE WOMAN IN WHITE

The Woman in White consists of a series of narratives and other documents ostensibly collected and 'edited' by Walter Hartright, and made to tell, among other things, 'the story of what a Woman's patience can endure, and of what a Man's resolution can achieve' (*WW* 1). This collection of narratives, like those of *No Name* and *The Moonstone*, originates in a legal lack; in this case it stands in for testimony in a court of law. It tells the story of how the protagonists (especially the editor/hero Walter Hartright) have acted on their own behalf to right various wrongs without the formal assistance of the law, since 'the Law is still . . . the pre-engaged servant of the long purse' (*WW* 1).

Marriage and the hierarchical, patriarchal, nuclear family (often in a deviant or disrupted form), and the social, psychological, moral and legal institutions that sustain these cornerstones of respectable Victorian society, are at the centre of all of Collins's novels. *The Woman in White*, like Collins's other sensation narratives, charts the transitions and transactions, within and across generations, between various fatherless and/or motherless families en route to (re-)establishing the normative companionate two-parent family of the bourgeois domestic ideal; a social and emotional unit in which both husband and wife find their vocation and their gender identity. However, before this destination is reached, both marriage and the family and the gender roles which they reproduce, and by which they are reproduced, are subjected to rigorous scrutiny.

Like virtually all sensation novels, *The Woman in White* is a critique of the mercenary marriage. Much of the plot is taken up with Sir Percival Glyde's attempts to ensure that Laura Fairlie complies with her dead father's wish that she should marry him, and with his subsequent machinations to obtain total control of her money and property. Although this particular mercenary marriage is associated with the dark plottings of a melodramatic villain (and his Italian accomplice, Count Fosco, one of the most insidiously fascinating villains of nineteenth-century fiction), it is in other respects far from extraordinary. As Marian Halcombe, Laura's half-sister, explains to Hartright early in the narrative, Laura is 'in the position of hundreds of other women, who marry men without being greatly attracted to them or greatly repelled by them, and who learn to love them (when they don't learn to hate!) after marriage instead of before' (*WW* 62).

In opposition to its mercenary marriage plot *The Woman in White* offers a counter-narrative, which is replicated in Victorian novels of all kinds; the story of how virtuous love outwits the 'long purse', and of the process by which the poor man who loves the rich lady overcomes the problems of his lowly social status, the wishes of the lady's family and the machinations of her apparently aristocratic and wealthy (but dishonest and increasingly desperate) suitor/husband. This counter-narrative combines the quest and self-sacrificing tasks required of the hero of romance with the Victorian ethos of self-help. Before he wins her as his bride and returns with her to her family home, Collins's hero must rescue the heroine from the prison of her mercenary marriage, and together with her half-sister care for her in a chaste *ménage à trois* modelled on the lower-middle-class household.

Before he assumes the role of Laura's husband, Hartright must occupy the role of both father and brother, those crucial male relatives whose lack has made Laura particularly vulnerable to Glyde's schemes. Before the poor man can marry the lady, she must be stripped of her property and the trappings of her class:

> Forlorn and disowned, sorely tired and sadly changed; her beauty faded, her mind clouded; robbed of her station in the world . . . the devotion I

had promised . . . might be laid blamelessly, now, at those dear feet. In the right of her calamity . . . she was mine at last! Mine to support, to protect, to cherish, to restore. Mine to love and honour as father and brother both. Mine to vindicate through all risks and all sacrifices – through the hopeless struggles against Rank and Power. (*WW* 381)

Here, as is so often the case in the sensation novel, properly socialized masculinity is defined in relation to, even constructed upon, vulnerable, dependent femininity. Hartright hides Laura away, labours to provide for her, and ultimately seeks out her persecutor and harries him to the point of destruction. Hartright's reward in this sensation plot (as, indeed, in most Victorian novels) is both the girl and the money. Having thoroughly discredited the mercenary marriage Collins smuggles a version of it back in at the end, with Hartright as the husband of a Laura restored to her former beauty, and to rather more than her former wits, and as the father of Laura's child, the heir to Limmeridge.

At the centre of Walter's narrative, as at the centre of all sensation novels, is a woman with a secret, or several women with secrets. The chief of these is Anne Catherick, the mysterious woman in white, who, in the startling sensation scene near the beginning of the novel, seems to step out of Hartright's night thoughts as he walks home across Hampstead Heath. The woman in white and the complex network of her relations with the other characters is used to raise questions about the ways in which social and sexual identities are constructed and the categories within which they are formed. This strange deranged woman, and the manner of her representation, present an interpretative problem for the characters in the text and the readers of it. The presentation of the initial night-time apparition indicates the scope of this problem: Is she a ghost? A street-walker? Is she mad or bad or a victim? Is she a 'lady'? All of these questions run through Hartright's mind as 'every drop of blood in [his] body was brought to a stop by the touch of a hand laid lightly and suddenly on [his] shoulder' (*WW* 15).

> There was nothing wild, nothing immodest in her manner: it was quiet and self-controlled . . . not exactly the manner of a lady, and, at the same time, not the manner of a woman in the humblest rank of life . . . What sort of woman she was, and how she came to be out alone in the high-road, an hour after midnight, I altogether failed to guess. (*WW* 15–16)

For Hartright, the meeting with this questionable woman, 'whose character, whose story, whose objects in life, whose very presence by my side . . . were fathomless mysteries to me' (*WW* 18) precipitates an identity crisis: 'It was like a dream. Was I Walter Hartright? . . . Had I really left, little more than an hour since, the quiet, decent, conventionally-domestic atmosphere of my mother's cottage?' (*WW* 18).

One of the reasons that the woman in white presents a challenge to Walter's identity is that her appearance challenges and blurs the gender categories upon which masculine identity was constructed. Walter's divided response to the woman is indicative of the contradictions of her appearance. Walter initially responds as a chivalrous gentleman to those aspects of her appearance which signify respectable, middle-class femininity: self-control, vulnerability, guardedness, 'loneliness and helplessness'. Having helped her to avoid recapture, he is racked with guilt that he has let loose that uncaged femininity that it is the duty of every respectable man to control.

At Limmeridge House, as the drawing master to two young ladies, one of whom bears an uncanny resemblance to Anne Catherick, Walter's identity crisis becomes more acute. Here in a house whose nominal head is an emasculated invalid (Laura's uncle), and whose most resourceful member is a masculinized woman (Marian Halcombe), Hartright occupies the feminized role of the socially inferior artist:

> I had long since learnt to understand . . . as a matter of course, that my situation in life was considered a guarantee against any of my female pupils feeling more than the most ordinary interest in me, and that I was admitted among beautiful and captivating women much as a harmless domestic animal is admitted among them. (*WW* 54–5)

Fathoming the mysteries of the dubious and deranged woman in white, and working out her connection with Laura Fairlie, the pupil with whom he falls in love, becomes one of the means by which Walter's identity crisis is resolved, and by which he is fully socialized into a conventional masculine role. This is a matter of action, work and the discovery of a vocation. Walter, the artistic drifter, is forced by love and trouble to 'act for myself' (*WW* 578), and to labour for love and money. In so doing he finds a vocation and a social role. Ultimately, as the agent of Laura's restoration to a Limmeridge freed from the enervation of its legitimate heir, and the moral degeneration of the illegitimate aristocrat who seeks to usurp it, and as the father of the new heir, Walter acts as the renovator of both the family and the landed gentry.

The close physical resemblance of Laura and Anne is central to the plot of *The Woman in White*, as is the fact that they are, in fact, related. Their relationship as textual doubles is also central to the novel's investigation of the formation of gendered social and psychological identities. In its treatment of Laura and Anne, Collins's text exposes the way in which genteel femininity is constructed. Anne, the hypersensitive female, wandering the borderlands of sanity and insanity, is Laura without the social and economic advantages. Laura is the legitimate daughter of a gentleman, and as such is brought up in an excessively protective atmosphere to occupy a passive, childlike and dependent role, first in the paternal home and later as the wife of one who claims aristocratic birth. The distracted state of Anne Catherick (the illegitimate daughter of a gentleman, who has inherited the nervous debility of her father's family), is, in one sense, merely a heightened form of Laura's genteel femininity. In Anne's case conventional feminine dependence and passivity, in the absence of the social and familial framework which usually produce and sustain it, becomes a form of illness, an aberrant psychological state.

Collins's narrative is structured so as to close the social and psychological gap between Laura and Anne. Stripped of her social and legal identity by Glyde's plotting, Laura is also stripped of her psychological identity. After her rescue from the asylum it appears to Walter as if Laura has indeed become Anne:

> The fatal resemblance which I had once . . . shuddered at seeing, in idea only, was now a real and living resemblance which asserted itself before my own eyes. (*WW* 400)

Collins's text substitutes Laura for Anne, just as Glyde substitutes Laura for Anne in the lunatic asylum. Both before and after her incarceration, Laura's domestic situation is repeatedly compared with Anne's (and later her own) containment within the asylum. Amidst the stifling, enervated gentility of Limmeridge House, and the gothic terrors of Blackwater Park, Laura is just as much a prisoner as she (or Anne) is in the asylum. Ironically, even when she is liberated from the asylum and her husband's tyranny into the care of Hartright and Marian, Laura is still subject to strict controls and is kept more or less a prisoner for her own protection. Indeed,

Collins's novel depends for many of its effects on the similarities between the domestic regulation of women in the household and the regime of moral management practised in Victorian asylums modelled on the genteel home.[2]

If the action of *The Woman in White* is structured in terms of those conventional sensation plot devices of conspiracy, incarceration, duplicity, the detective hunt, the mysterious woman, and so on, this action is in turn organized around a series of pairings (which recur in virtually all of Collins's sensation narratives): sanity/insanity, legitimacy/illegitimacy, masculinity/femininity, genteel femininity/the fallen woman, the womanly woman/the unwomanly woman. Collins's narratives are driven by the dynamic interactions of these paired terms, and in many cases the novel's action turns on or explores the way the polarities are defined, and the confusions and ambiguities that lurk within them.

The borderline (and the borderland) between sanity and insanity lies at the heart of this novel, as it does, in some sense, in all of Collins's sensation novels. One of the most interesting aspects of Collins's representation of this borderland in *The Woman in White* is its inversion of the dominant code. The classic nineteenth-century madwoman is the deviant, energetic woman who defies familial and social control (a type which Collins was to use to great effect in later novels). In *The Woman in White*, however, it is the passive, controlled, domestic women (Anne and Laura) who are 'mad'. The sanity/insanity pairing is closely allied to the femininity/masculinity pairing, since, in the medical or psychiatric discourse within which Collins is working, madness is defined in relation to ideas of femininity. The indicators of insanity – feeling, excess, emotionalism, irrationality, histrionics – were also signifiers of femininity. Indeed, as Elaine Showalter has pointed out, madness in the nineteenth century was a 'female malady'.[3]

The Woman in White, like all of Collins's novels (I would argue, like all sensation novels) is shot through with anxieties and ambiguities about the masculinity/femininity pairing. It is deeply concerned with the blurring of the boundary between these two terms. This is potentially very subversive, since it exposes the ways in which this boundary is constructed within specific codes of representation and perception. Thus the reader's perception of Marian Halcombe's 'masculinity' is, in large measure, a product of Hartright's conventional perceptual framework through which Marian is mediated. Hartright sees Marian's body as a model of female beauty, but her 'large, firm, masculine mouth and jaw', swarthy complexion, dark down on the upper lip, 'prominent, piercing, resolute brown eyes' all signify masculinity. Even more alarming, 'her expression – bright, frank, and intelligent – appeared, while she was silent, to be altogether wanting in those feminine attractions of gentleness and pliability' (*WW* 25). What is attractive in a woman is, in terms of the dominant codes of representation, repulsive in a man. Hartright's perception of Frederick Fairlie, Laura's uncle, is the logical extension of his view of Marian. His 'beardless face', 'effeminately small feet', 'little womanish' slippers, his 'frail, languidly-fretful, over-refined look' had 'something singularly and unpleasantly delicate in its association with a man' (*WW* 32).

The perceptual codes by which gender difference is constructed are also explored via Marian Halcombe's diaries. Here the world is viewed through the eyes of a woman who questions and refuses the dominant codes. She chafes under the restraints of her 'petticoat existence', fulminates against men as 'the enemies of our [women's] innocence and our peace', and observes with a critical and knowing eye the transformation (by a man and marriage) of the vain, opinionated Eleanor Fairlie to a 'civil, silent, unobtrusive woman, who is never in the way' (*WW* 195). Through Collins's use of different narratorial perspectives we are confronted with different ways of seeing gender difference. This creates a space in which the reader can see that these are, for the most part, *just* ways of seeing: gender is not something natural and fixed, but produced and subject to change. This is either immensely liberating, or it induces deep anxiety, depending on the reader's point of view. I think that in the end this subversive potential is (on the whole) contained and a normative view of masculinity/femininity is restored. The world of *The Woman in White* seems to be one in which the relation between masculinity and femininity has somehow gone wrong. It has both masculinized women and feminized men, but mostly there is just too much femininity around, and where there is masculinity it occurs in inappropriate places. One of the things that Collins's narrative does is to redress this gender imbalance.

Another imbalance that is redressed in *The Woman in White* is that between legitimacy and illegitimacy. This pairing, like all the other pairings in this novel, is inextricably tied up with the question of gender and gender stereotypes. The key figure here is the fallen woman, since illegitimacy, by definition, involves an unmarried mother (or a married woman who has a child that is not her husband's). The plot of *The Woman in White* originates in illegitimacy: the illegitimacy of Glyde and of Anne Catherick. Mrs Catherick, a fallen woman, is the link between the different plot strands. Again there is the suggestion of a disruptive femininity let loose on the world. As in so many sensation novels, one of the narrative goals of this novel is to (re-)establish the (legally) legitimate succession, and to establish its moral legitimacy. Thus, at the end of the novel, the legal heirs of Limmeridge succeed to what is rightfully theirs. 'Succeed' and 'rightful' here have a moral as well as a legal meaning: they have succeeded by their own efforts, and their right is that of moral authority. Squaring the circle of moral and legal legitimacy and containing disruptive femininity is also a major concern of Collins's next novel.

NO NAME

In *The Woman in White* the marriage and property laws are used and manipulated to strip the heroine of her property, status, and even her identity. In *No Name* it is the 'heroine' (if one may use this term for its transgressive central female character) who resorts to marriage scheming in order to regain the name and property which the law has taken away. Like its predecessor *No Name* originates in a crisis of legitimacy, and foregrounds the problematic legal status and economic dependency of women.

In *No Name* the Vanstone family is quite literally destroyed when the sudden deaths of their parents reveal Norah and Magdalen Vanstone to be illegitimate. The death of Mr Vanstone's wife, a disreputable woman who had tricked him into marriage when he was a young soldier in Canada, had finally permitted the Vanstone parents to legalize their union only weeks before they themselves met with unexpected deaths. Like Sir Percival Glyde (whose secret illegitimacy is a powerful narrative force in *The Woman in White*) the Vanstone sisters have no legal right to their name, their place in society, or (because of a legal nicety about the dating of a will) their father's property, which passes to an unsympathetic male relative. The Vanstone sisters are the victims of what Miss Garth (their former governess) describes as 'a cruel law', which 'visits the sins of the parents on the children', and is 'a disgrace to the nation' (*NN* 98).

Collins's preoccupation with illegitimacy and inheritance may be explained, in part, by the irregularity of his own domestic arrangements; he never married, but maintained separate households with Caroline Graves and Martha Rudd, also known as 'Mrs Dawson', the mother of his three children (see William M. Clarke in Bibliography). However, it is also part of a more general investigation of the ways in which the law's intervention in family life defines and restricts those whom it claims to protect – especially women.

The opening chapters of *No Name* offer a picture of domestic bliss and well-ordered family life which is destroyed by the discovery that the Vanstones were not in fact married for almost all of the twenty-seven years of their partnership. The almost perfect happy family to which the reader has been introduced is revealed retrospectively to be no family at all in the legal sense. Thus, from the outset, a tension is set up between the idea of the family as an affective emotional space, and as a socio-legal institution. The discovery of the legal irregularity also casts the shadow of impropriety over a family which has hitherto been a model of respectability. This plot device triggers an exploration and interrogation of the codes of propriety and respectability, which is an important part of this novel's project.

The sudden shift in family fortunes with which *No Name* begins is a common device in sensation fiction and derives from a broader cultural anxiety about the stability of the family. This anxiety is partly economic: the women sensation novelists were particularly concerned with the financial insecurities of the higher classes of society. It is also based on mid-century uncertainties about the nature, structure and function of the family as a social institution. Even before the revelations which destroy the Vanstone family there are indications of familial instability and disturbance in Magdalen's excess of feeling, her impulsiveness, her disregard for social proprieties, her delight in exercising her talent for acting, and her playful subversion of her father's authority. From the outset disruptive femininity threatens the family. There is an interesting displacement at work here. On one level Collins's narrative makes it clear that the disaster which befalls the Vanstone sisters is the result of an unjust law and the selfishness of a male relative. However, the novel's focusing on Magdalen's excessive emotions and her scheming also has the effect of transferring the reader's attention, and perhaps also the blame for the family's predicament, onto her perverse femininity and her obsessive desire for revenge and restitution.

Magdalen is a particularly striking example of the sensation novel's concern with – or perhaps it would be more accurate to describe it as an anxiety about – feminine duplicity. At times the sensation novel seems to *define* femininity *as* duplicity and to represent respectable, genteel femininity as impersonation, performance or masquerade. This novel uses acting as a general metaphor for social existence. It also explores the complexities and problems of a concept of identity based on performance. Magdalen is represented as a 'natural' or 'born' actress. Significantly her 'habits of mimicry' (*NN* 8) and her talent for acting (demonstrated in the private theatricals in chapters 5 and 6) are linked to her vivacity and love of sensation:

> I want to go to another concert . . . anything that puts me into a new dress, and plunges me into a crowd of people, and illuminates me with plenty of light, and sets me in a tingle of excitement all over, from head to foot. (*NN* 7–8)

When she is deprived of her legal identity and her place in respectable middle-class society, Magdalen both reacts and acts: she reacts with violent emotion to injustice, and she acts in the sense of taking positive steps to deal with her changed circumstances. She does not merely regret the restraints of petticoat existence, as Marian Halcombe does, she refuses to accept them. She is the antithesis of the respectable feminine ideal, personified by the passive, accepting Laura Fairlie and by her own sister; she is 'resolute and impetuous, clever and domineering . . . not one of those model women who want a man to look up to and protect them' (*NN* 52). (Although, of course, before her drama is played out she will be required to be saved from her own excesses and to rely on the protection of a strong man.)

Magdalen adapts to the loss of her original social status by transgressing the code of propriety and working as a professional actress in the public theatre. She also takes on a fluid and changing identity as she deliberately impersonates a series of different social roles. In Magdalen, Collins creates a character who demonstrates the instability of the particular conception of (respectable, middle-class) feminine identity which underpins the dominant code of social propriety, and also the contradictions inherent in that code.

Magdalen performs this function by self-consciously exploiting her perception that 'a lady is a woman who wears a silk gown, and has a sense of her own importance' (*NN* 453). In one sense Magdalen's scheming is but a heightened version of the machinations in which thousands of middle-class women (and men) engaged in order to make a good marriage: 'Thousands of women marry for money . . . Why shouldn't I?' (*NN* 361). Through scheming and impersonation, and by making 'the general sense of propriety my accomplice' (*NN* 436), Magdalen acquires, if only briefly, a legitimate social identity:

> I am a respectable married woman . . . I have got a place in the world, and a name in the world, at last. Even the law which is the friend of all you respectable people, has recognised my existence, and has become my friend too . . . my wickedness has made Nobody's Child, Somebody's Wife. (*NN* 436)

Two things distinguish Magdalen from her sister Norah and the thousands of other 'respectable' women (less noble than the saintly Norah) who play the required social role and succeed in marrying for money. One is the extraordinary self-conscious exploitativeness of her performance, the other is the multiplicity of parts she plays. These two distinguishing characteristics are the marks of Magdalen's excess, of the perversity which I mentioned earlier. In Collins's representation of Magdalen, the histrionic and the hysterical are closely connected: Magdalen's acting is produced by and induces hysteria, that excessive emotional state into which, according to nineteenth-century medical discourse, all women were perpetually in danger of falling.

Collins's narrative is driven by the energy of Magdalen's transgressive excess. Norah's 'story', on the other hand, demonstrates that good women do not have a story, they inhabit a sub-plot. However, if Magdalen's excess is the source of narrative, the curtailment of that excess is its end; that is to say it is both the goal of the narrative and its closure. Magdalen's adoption of multiple identities as the means of regaining (regressing to?) her original identity results in self-fragmentation and a loss of social, legal and psychological identity. All of Magdalen's schemes are frustrated, and she retires from the fray penniless and exhausted. The final part of the novel depicts Magdalen's decline into a life-threatening nervous collapse and physical illness, from which she is rescued by Captain Kirke, the sailor whom she had unwittingly encountered at a crucial earlier stage in her moral development (or degeneration). Intriguingly, the agent of Magdalen's restoration to respectable society and her reclamation for the patriarchal family is the son of her father's closest friend from his Canadian days. Magdalen emerges from her illness not with a restored identity, but with an identity which has been reshaped by her recognition of herself as the woman who is loved by Captain Kirke – a man who nurses her with a woman's tenderness – and by her recognition of Kirke as the man she would have liked to have been: 'Oh, if I could be a man, how I should like to be such a man as this!' (*NN* 533).

Magdalen is a particularly powerful version of the new self-assertive, independent heroine for which the sensation novel was renowned (or infamous). She is one of those 'bouncing, ill-conditioned, impudent young [women]', whose fictional rise Collins noted in 'A Petition to the Novel-Writers' (*My Miscellanies*, 1863, 66). Collins represents this new stereotype with an ambivalence which is characteristic of the sensation genre. Collins's text positions its readers so that we cannot entirely condone Magdalen, but nor can we unequivocally condemn her. Instead we are made into the spectators of her beauty and brilliance, and the witnesses of her emotional turmoil. Throughout the narrative Magdalen is defined as a woman of feeling. An excess of self-assertive, self-directed feeling is the origin of her moral decline. On the other hand, the vulnerable feminine sensitivity which follows her hysterical breakdown, and (finally) properly directed (heterosexual) feeling are the means by which she is reclaimed. I shall return to the matter of the representation and circulation of feminine feeling in the sensation novel, and the questions it raises, when I look at the female sensationalists.

ARMADALE

The transgressive heroine is taken several stages further in Lydia Gwilt, the *femme fatale* villainess of *Armadale*, a novel about greed, cupidity, jealousy and fatalism. The actions of Braddon's Lady Audley (hitherto the type of the beautiful and deceptively demure sensation villainess) pale into insignificance beside the passionate intensity and sophisticated, scheming criminality of Lydia Gwilt. This attractive governess, murderess, adulteress and forger is the extreme form of the demonic sensation heroine, 'at once passionate and cold-blooded, resolute and capable of murder'.[4] She conceals both her emotional intensity and her criminality beneath the façade of the respectable Victorian lady.

> Perfectly modest in her manner, possessed to perfection of the graceful refinements of a lady, she had all the allurements that feast the eye, all the siren-invitations that seduce the sense – a subtle suggestiveness in her silence and a sexual sorcery in her smile. (*A* 373)

Once more the central female character of a sensation novel is double, and the novel exploits the fear that the self-sacrificing, passionless gentility which constitutes the feminine ideal is merely a form of acting or impersonation which masks female passion and self-interest. The story that the character attempts to write for herself is a ruthless self-help narrative aimed at securing a stable social and financial position by exploiting her sexual attractiveness and successfully impersonating respectable femininity. The story that Collins writes for her involves the exposure of her impersonation and the revelation of the duplicity and intense passions which it masks. Collins does this by giving the reader a privileged access to his character's inner dramas by using Lydia's diary, and letters between Lydia and her partner in crime, the procuress Mother Oldershaw.

These documents allow the reader to watch Lydia watching herself (as do Marian Halcombe's diaries in *The Woman in White*). They present the reader with a particular form of the self-surveillance upon which Victorian identity and morality were founded. In the letters, and more especially the diary, Lydia is revealed as a complex and contradictory mixture of calculating rationality and impulsive emotionalism, coolheadedness and obsessiveness, sexual desire and sexual disgust (for example, when she remembers her past history of sexual degradation). The letters and diary also chart the process by which Lydia demonstrates her capacity for redemption. Once more feeling is the key. Misplaced (perverse) desire is the source of Lydia's transgressiveness. On the other hand, as her diary shows, properly directed feeling (spontaneous, romantic, heterosexual love) is the possible route to repentance. Lydia's love for Midwinter becomes a form of conscience. Interestingly her love for Midwinter not only deflects Lydia from her schemes, it also deflects her from her self-obsession; the strong, resourceful, independent woman is made vulnerable and dependent by sexual desire and romantic love.

It is not possible, however, for the sensation novel to envisage the reincorporation into respectable society of a character whose criminality is as varied and as profound as Lydia Gwilt's. Many critics, including Margaret Oliphant, had been outraged by the rescue of Magdalen Vanstone from 'a career of vulgar and aimless trickery and wickedness', at the apparently 'cheap cost of a fever', from which she emerges 'as pure, as high-minded and as spotless as the most dazzling white of heroines'.[5] In *Armadale* the possibility of a moral redemption is signalled by the *femme fatale's* final act of self-sacrifice, when she saves Midwinter's life by sacrificing her own. In its fantasy resolution of the problem of the deadly woman, Collins's novel turns the destructive potential of transgressive femininity against itself.

Lydia Gwilt is at the centre of the text from which she is, in the end, violently expelled. Her own schemes and her association with such figures as Mother Oldershaw and Doctor Downward (also known as Le Doux, an abortionist turned proprietor of a sanatorium for nervous invalids) place her at the heart of Collins's critique of the cupidity, corruption and criminality which lurks within respectable Victorian society. She is also at the centre (as both victim and instigator) of that network of surveillance and spying which the novel represents as the characteristic form of modern life. Spying and being spied on are among the dominant activities in sensation fiction. Spying is clearly the other side of the sensation novel's concern with secrecy, and its suggestion that everyone has something to hide. At the centre of the insidious and pervasive network of surveillance is 'the Confidential Spy of modern times . . . the necessary detective attendant on the progress of our national civilization . . . a man professionally ready on the merest suspicion (if the merest suspicion paid him) to get under our beds, and to look through gimlet-holes in our doors' (*A* 506). This fictional preoccupation with surveillance and detection, and the rise of the detective and detective fiction have been described by Walter Benjamin as symptoms of urban modernity. As he observes of nineteenth-century Paris: 'in times of terror, when everyone is something of a conspirator, everybody will be in a situation where he has to play detective'.[6]

Lydia also plays a crucial role in the fatal inheritance plot which gives rise to many of the novel's most thrilling sensation scenes. Many of the proliferating plots of this extraordinarily complexly plotted novel radiate out from the story of family secrets which is told in the confessional narrative contained in the novel's Prologue. This Prologue establishes the novel's concern with questions of identity, and with inheritance – of a name and property. It also raises questions about the determining influence of the familial past, whether through the transmission of degenerative physical and mental characteristics, or as a shaping destiny or fate.

The Prologue tells a story of intra-familial conflict and murder in the form of the (dictated) confession of Allan Armadale to his son, also Allan Armadale. The dying Armadale (originally named Wrentmore) confesses to the murder of the man whose name he had been required to take as a condition of inheriting the Armadale property in England and Barbados. This confession is both a testament of guilt and a prophecy of its ineradicability:

> I see danger in the future, begotten of the danger in the past – treachery that is the offspring of *his* treachery, and crime that is the child of *my* crime . . . I see the vices which have contaminated the father, descending and contaminating the child . . . (*A* 39–40)

The confession ends with a prophetic warning to his son:

> Avoid the widow of the man I killed . . . Avoid the maid whose wicked hand smoothed the way to the marriage . . . avoid the man who bears the same name as your own . . . hide yourself from him under an assumed name . . . be all that is most repellent to your own gentler nature, rather than live under the same roof . . . with that man. (*A* 40–1)

The reader of a psychoanalytic bent will no doubt find much to ponder in this Law of the Father which (as it turns out) forbids relationships with the very man and woman whom the son most desires.

The confession is given a central role in the novel's investigation of the processes by which identity and subjectivity are formed. When Wrentmore/Armadale's son reads these words in the letter of confession that is part of his inheritance when he comes of age, they give a retrospective shape and meaning to the painful puzzle of his existence:

> there was I, an ill-conditioned brat, with my mother's negro blood in my face, and my murdering father's passions in my heart. (*A* 81–2)

When he reads the confession, the murderer's son has already changed his name to Ozias Midwinter in the course of a wandering self-exile from his family. The confession produces further complications in Midwinter's sense of identity. It leads to both a repudiation of self and an acceptance of the guilt and unworthiness which has been imposed upon him by his father. This re-formation of Midwinter's identity is also accompanied by a process of splitting. His knowledge of the guilty past, and his fears about its ability to shape the future lead Midwinter to spy upon himself, in other words to practise a form of that self-surveillance I noted in Lydia Gwilt.

Midwinter's hypersensitivity, his susceptibility to non-rational modes of interpretation, and his emotional self-policing combine to place him in a role in the sensation narrative more usually occupied by a female character – the hysteric. His hysterical symptoms are the result of a desire to repress and to control his fears and feelings (in other words, to be 'manly'). They are the result too of the withdrawal from emotional bonds which he imposes upon himself in an attempt both to outwit and to deny the version of history contained in his father's prophecy. Ironically, however, each time that Midwinter scores a 'victory over his own fatalism' he seems to open a door to further crime, and the Armadale curse seems to move one more stage towards fulfilment. Significantly the chief instigator of this crime is Lydia Gwilt, who as a 12-year-old servant had played a part in the dramas of the earlier generation of Allan Armadales. The repressed legacy of the past thus re-enters the narrative, as it so often does in sensation fiction, in the shape of a guilty, powerful and sexually desirable woman.

The cycle of guilt and treachery is only broken by means of Midwinter's confronting and expelling Lydia Gwilt and by his confronting and redirecting the feminine in himself – he 'take[s] to Literature' (A 660). In the process the links with the West Indies – that wild zone of dissolute youth, and financial and sexual speculation and intrigue – are finally severed. The name of Allan Armadale becomes fixed to a member of the English aristocracy and owner of the thoroughly modern Thorpe Ambrose, 'a purely conventional country-house – the product of the classical idea filtered judiciously through the commercial English mind' (A 161). The novel's ending, like that of many other sensation novels, is *diminuendo*. It concludes with a peculiarly (and rather enfeebled) English tranquillity, with the wedding of Allan Armadale, a model of frank, open, English masculinity, to the ultra-feminine, respectably insipid, 'Neelie' Milroy.

THE MOONSTONE

The plot of *The Moonstone* like that of *Armadale* also originates in a tale of violence and greed in the colonies, and in the familial discord of an earlier generation. This tale is also told in a Prologue (a document from the Herncastle family papers) which relates the history of the Yellow Diamond, 'a famous gem in the native annals of India' (*M* 33), and of its removal to England from its latest resting place in Seringapatam. As in *Armadale*, the main narrative of *The Moonstone* concerns the disruption of the tranquillity and order of genteel English life by a colonial legacy. The Diamond and its attendant burdens are left to Rachel Verinder in the will of her uncle (who had plundered the Diamond in battle) as an act of vengeance against the family which had ostracized him. In the 'political unconscious' of this text (to use Fredric Jameson's term,[7]) Rachel's inheritance of the Diamond also signifies the inescapability and pervasiveness of the burden of colonial guilt; even genteel young women are implicated in the white man's burden, and the consequences of colonial plunder surface in the English country house. As the loquacious Gabriel Betteredge, the Verinder's loyal family servant puts it:

> by a devilish Indian Diamond . . . Who ever heard the like of it – in the nineteenth century mind; in an age of progress, and in a country that rejoices in the blessings of the British constitution. (*M* 67)

This, the most domestic of Collins's novels, involves a crime at the very heart and hearth of the family. Indeed there has been a great deal of debate as to whether *The Moonstone* should be considered as a sensation novel at all, or whether it should more properly be seen as a prototype of the detective novel, and one of the earliest occurrences of the English Country House Mystery. Certainly it has many of the features that became staple ingredients of the Country House Mystery: the crime is committed at a family gathering – the celebration of Rachel's birthday – which brings together a mixed group of people, many of whom might have a motive for committing the crime; it has suspicious servants; there is a bumbling local policeman (Seegrave) whose dullness of wit and lack of gentility render him quite unequipped to decipher the codes of the genteel household; a detective of repute (Cuff), more used to the ways of the gentry, is brought in to apply his specialist intuitive as well as

31

deductive skills to the mystery (only in this case he comes to the wrong conclusion in the first instance).

Whatever its claims to be the protypical English detective novel, *The Moonstone* certainly has many of the key components of sensation fiction: (1) it makes use of dreams and altered states of consciousness; (2) it produces thrills by means of atmospheric writing (most notably in the descriptions of the Shivering Sands); (3) it turns on a mystery from the past; (4) family secrets lie at its centre; (5) there is a marriage plot and fraud, both perpetrated by the same individual; (6) there is a minute focus on the domestic space and domestic relations; (7) the amateur detective is a young man (Franklin Blake) with foreign tastes and no clearly defined social role, and hence no clearly defined gender role; (8) a crucial part is played by a woman with a guilty past and a present secret – Rosanna Spearman, who has been imprisoned for theft, and who cherishes a hopeless love for a man who is her social superior; (9) the narrative is kept in motion by a woman with a secret (Rachel Verinder); (10) female passions propel the narrative, and female passions and physical sensations are minutely described.

Rachel Verinder, as Collins's Preface makes clear, is at the centre of *The Moonstone*: 'the conduct pursued, under a sudden emergency, by a young girl, supplies the foundation on which I have built this book' (*M* 28). The theft of the Diamond disrupts the Verinder household and gives rise to the 'detective fever' around which the plot is constructed, but it is Rachel's 'conduct' (and also Sergeant Cuff's misreading of her conduct) which keeps that plot in motion. The mystery of the disappearance of the Diamond becomes submerged in the mystery of Rachel's conduct. In effect Rachel also goes missing – by means of her silence, her strangely altered behaviour to Franklin, her self-incarceration in her room and subsequent removal from her home, and by means of the hysteria which is represented as 'an absence of all ladylike restraint in her language and manner' (*M* 244). Rachel thus becomes the mystery, the puzzle to be solved, and the cherished object that is restored to its domestic setting after careful detective work.

In Rachel we encounter yet again that collocation of female assertiveness and hysteria which we saw in Magdalen Vanstone. Rachel's strange 'conduct . . . under a sudden emergency' is simply an extension of that 'defect' of 'secrecy and self-will' (*M* 87) which makes her 'odd and wild' (*M* 262), and marks her everyday conduct as different from other girls of her class and age.

> *She was unlike most other girls of her age, in this that she had ideas of her own,* and was stiff-necked enough to set the fashions themselves at defiance, if the fashions did not suit her views. In trifles, this independence of hers was well enough; but in matters of importance, it carried her (as my lady thought, and as I thought) too far. She judged for herself . . . never told you beforehand what she was going to do; never came with secrets and confidences . . . [and] always went on a way of her own. (*M* 87, my emphasis)

Self-will, independence, ideas of her own, the desire to judge for herself, keeping her own counsel, disregard for convention – these markers of Rachel's distinctiveness from other girls are also the signs of Eliza Lynn Linton's 'Girl of the Period', that embodiment of mid-Victorian fears about the nature of modern femininity, who first appeared in the *Saturday Review* in 1868 (i.e. the same year as *The Moonstone*).

Collins's representation of Rachel is deeply ambivalent. It is full of the contradictions that characterized nineteenth-century discourses on femininity, and especially on feminine feeling. Although they are constantly perceived as 'odd' and 'wild' by her family and friends, Rachel's secrecy, her self-dependence and exceptional self-control are, in a sense only heightened versions of those virtues of self-containment, modesty and restraint which were universally recommended to respectable middle-class women, and were, indeed, the defining characteristics of domestic femininity. Rachel's real secret, however, is that her self-containment and self-control mask her fear of a fundamental lack of control, and an inability to contain her feelings, especially her feelings for Franklin Blake.

While the male characters work to detect the thief, Rachel is engaged in a psychic drama of detecting what she perceives as the awful truth about herself: that she cannot 'tear from [her] heart' her love for a man she knows (on the evidence of her own eyes) to be unworthy. This guilty secret is a peculiarly feminine one:

> Oh, how can I find words to say it in! How can I make *a man* understand that a feeling which horrifies me at myself, can be a feeling that fascinates me at the same time? (*M* 279)

The drama of Rachel's feelings and sensations, as with most sensation heroines, is displayed as a spectacle to the reader, and is the source of some of the novel's most sensational writing. The climax of this drama occurs in chapter 7 of 'The Discovery of the Truth', in which (at least as seen from the perspective of Franklin Blake, the narrator of this section) Rachel is in thrall to her feelings. For most of this chapter she is represented as moving automatically, propelled by the messages of the body, mesmerized by the sound of Franklin's voice, and mastered by his touch. The result is an orgy of hysterical self-abasement:

> 'I am worse, if worse can be, than you are yourself.' Sobs and tears burst from her. She struggled with them fiercely . . . 'I can't tear you out of my heart . . . even now! you may trust in the shameful, shameful weakness which can only struggle against you in this way! . . . O God! I despise myself even more heartily than I despise *him*!' (*M* 403)

This chapter plays on the readers' contradictory fears and desires about femininity. It displays the spectacle of the exquisite anguish of Rachel's 'illicit' passion for a man who she 'knows' to be unworthy of the love of a respectable woman, for the delight of a reader who knows that the man in the case is honourable.

Another version of the spectacle of female passion is found in the letter in which Rosanna Spearman declares her love for Franklin Blake. In Rosanna's case, as in Rachel's a woman's passion is associated with secrecy and silence, but it is given a different class inflection. Rachel, a representative (however disordered) of genteel femininity, retreats into silence to protect the reputation of the man she loves (and perhaps also because she does not wish to expose her own guilt in having loved an apparent criminal). The respectability of middle-class masculinity is thus preserved by the self-sacrificing silence of a colluding woman. On the other hand, the servant Rosanna sees her silence as a direct form of power, and a potential means of closing the class gap. (The reward for Rachel's collusion is marriage, the price of Rosanna's delusion is self-destruction.)

The intersections of class and gender are particularly important in the novel's central plot situation, the crisis in the family and household. The nineteenth-century household was defined as a predominantly feminine space. The ideal of femininity and the ideal of domesticity were each defined in terms of the other. However, if the woman (as wife and mother) was the queen of the domestic domain and keeper of the household temple, the home and household were also the means of containing and controlling both women and those feared aspects of femininity that were suppressed by the domestic ideal. *The Moonstone* calls attention to the family's role in policing femininity by its use of Sergeant Cuff, the family policeman, who, 'for the last twenty years . . . [has] been largely employed in cases of family scandal, acting in the capacity of confidential man' (*M* 205). Cuff's role (and it is one he quite self-consciously pursues) is to seek out the criminal secrets of the family, and to contain them 'within the family limits' (*M* 208). As this outsider informs the insider Betteredge, 'I have put my muzzle on worse family difficulties than this in my time' (*M* 171). Cuff's success derives largely from his practice of getting the family to police itself: 'The less noise made, and the fewer strangers employed . . . the better' (*M* 208). The evidence of Cuff's 'domestic practice' (*M* 205) and the assumption on which it is based is that the family is a prime site of criminality. However, his genteel clients project the dis-ease of the family onto the detective, as in Lady Verinder's 'presentiment that he is bringing trouble and misery with him into the house' (*M* 143). For the nineteenth-century reader the sensation plot was, very often, a way of displacing various kinds of uneasiness about the dis-ease of the family.

Cuff's flawed expertise as the policeman of the family plays a vital part in keeping the mystery narrative in process. Cuff is defeated by the silence of women (Rachel and Rosanna), by feminine reticence (Lady Verinder), and the failure of individual women to conform to dominant stereotypes of femininity. Cuff retires from the fray having correctly concluded that Rachel is the key to the mystery, but having falsely diagnosed the nature of the mystery. His misdiagnosis is the result of his over-confidence in the lessons of his 'domestic practice', which leads to his misreading of the signs of Rachel Verinder's conduct. His mistake is to subsume the particular woman into the generality 'Woman', and to assume that all 'young ladies of rank and position' (*M* 205) are the same.

Despite his experience of the family and young ladies, Cuff is wrong-footed because, as a lower-class man, he is unable, finally, to understand the upper-middle-class family and the genteel femininity upon which it is predicated. Cuff and, for that matter, the Verinder family lawyer Bruff huff and puff good-naturedly but leaden-footedly around the subject of woman, unable to fathom her mysteries. They are the comic side of *The Moonstone*'s preoccupation (again, it's a common concern of the sensation novel) with the problematic relationship of men to the feminine space of the affective family (as opposed to the family as legal, economic entity).

The manner in which Franklin Blake and Godfrey Ablewhite are depicted, and their roles in the sensation plot also throw interesting light on the sensation novel's concern with men, masculinity and the family. The blurring of gender categories that we noted in the feminized lower-middle-class artist Hartright, and the hystericized (and hence feminized) déclassé Ozias Midwinter, are also evident in Blake and Ablewhite. Ablewhite, as it turns out, is a ladies' man in the usually accepted sense, but for most of the novel he is portrayed as quite a different kind of ladies' man. This smooth-shaven man with his 'head of lovely long flaxen hair, falling negligently over the poll of his neck' (M 89) has thoroughly penetrated the world of female philanthropy, and serves as the lone male on all its committees. Franklin Blake's ambivalent gender status, on the other hand, is connected with his unconventional (i.e. not English public school) and dilettante foreign education, and his lack of a clearly defined social role. The son of a wealthy man who aspires to a dukedom, he pursues a somewhat outdated aristocratic mode of living and has no professional training or vocation. He is one of several sensation heroes who indulge a taste for French novels and German philosophy while waiting to come into their father's money. 'He wrote a little; he painted a little; he sang and composed a little' (M 48) whilst leading a nomadic existence and borrowing and giving money in a 'lively, easy way' (M 48).

Although, as I have argued, it is feminine passion and the mystery of feminine silence that keep this sensation narrative in process, it is these two feminized males who start it off. Franklin has the role of 'messenger' since it is he who brings the Diamond into the house, and Franklin and Godfrey both play a part in its disappearance. In Franklin's case the disappearance of the Diamond is the first stage in the process by which he becomes fully socialized and masculinized. Franklin becomes caught up in the 'detective fever' which pervades this narrative, but his search for the thief of the Diamond is but a means to another end. It is, in fact, a quest: a task he sets himself, in the manner of the romance hero, to prove himself worthy of his lady's love; a quest to fathom the mystery of his lady, 'to find out the secret of her silence towards her mother, and her enmity towards *me*' (M 343). Blake's quest also turns out to be a quest for identity, both his own and Rachel's. His detective work produces a crisis of personal identity. It also involves him in plumbing the depths of his own and Rachel's unconscious, when he submits to replaying the events of the night of the Diamond's disappearance, and when he acts as a kind of psychoanalyst to Rachel, compelling her to tell the story of what she saw in the bedroom (a kind of primal scene). The end of the quest, and the resolution of the mystery is not (as one might have expected) the discovery of the Diamond, but the discovery of the 'true' identities of Franklin and Rachel as the renovators of the family through romantic love and companionate marriage.

The final destination of this narrative, like all sensation novels (indeed like most mid-Victorian novels) is marriage. However, the end of the *narration* serves to reinsert this romantic marriage into the complex context of Victorian sexual customs. The ending of *The Moonstone* foregrounds the way in which respectable Victorian marriage and genteel femininity were defined in terms of, and indeed constructed in relation to, prostitution and fallen women. When we read the cynically narrated story of Ablewhite's domestic arrangements and his secret life in the suburbs (and it is interesting to note that it is Sergeant Cuff, the policeman of the respectable family, who is the cynical narrator here), we may perhaps be led to the conclusion that the real disrupter of 'our quiet English house' was not the Diamond, but a fallen woman – the kept 'lady in the villa', 'such familiar objects in London life' (*M* 506–7).

DOING THE POLICE IN DIFFERENT VOICES

The narrative structure and methods of narration of sensation novels are organized around concealment and the prolongation of mystery and suspense in a kind of 'narrative hide-and-seek'.[8] In Collins's sensation novels this game of narrative hide-and-seek was pursued by means of multiple narrators, or by the creation of multiple-narrator effects through the use of letters, journals and other documents. Collins's use of multiple narrators with their linked and overlapping narratives creates an impression of verisimilitude or actuality. The use of separate narrators permits a range of different voices to be heard, speaking from different social and gender perspectives. Servants and lower-class characters add their voices and stories to those of their masters, mistresses and other social superiors. Women's voices are heard, sometimes talking to themselves (in diaries and journals) and sometimes talking to other women (in letters). The documents and personal accounts that make up Collins's narratives are forms of testimony, which sometimes read like the evidence of witnesses in a court of law, or the 'I was there' school of journalism. They are also used to give a privileged access to a character's interiority.

However, although the individual narratives have the authority that comes from direct observation and experience, and bear many of the marks of realism, it is not the totalizing realism that we tend to associate with the mid-Victorian novel. The separate narratives are not only individual, they are also quite clearly idiosyncratic, subjective, quirky and partial. They are also limited; each particular narrator only knows part of the story, or, as in the case of *The Woman in White* and *The Moonstone*, is under strict instructions to confine him- or herself to what he or she actually experienced.

Collins's narrative method results in the fragmentation of narrative and the dispersal of narrative authority. Instead of the utterance of the sagacious, omniscient narrator of the realist novel, we have a heap of fragments, linked either by the invisible hand of the impersonal narrator in *No Name* and *Armadale*, or by the editorializing of Hartright in *The Woman in White* and Blake in *The Moonstone*. In the last two cases there *is* a kind of totalizing vision, but its imperative is subjective – the desire of the hero/detective/narrator to assert his mastery over experience and events by making them tell his story: a story of rationality, causality and control.

These aspects of the sensation narrative may be seen as symptomatic of a crisis of narrative authority in the mid-nineteenth-century novel, and also of wider cultural developments. The fragmentation of the narrative voice, and/or the unreliability of the third-person narrator in Collins's novels (and perhaps in sensation fiction more generally), is related to what Raymond Williams has called the disappearance of the 'knowable community'.[9] The fiction of the earlier part of the nineteenth century represented a world that was presumed to be 'knowable', which could be held together and comprehended by a single consciousness. For example, Jane Austen with her 'two or three families in a country village' preserved the fiction of a community which could still be known and possessed by an omniscient narrator. The growth of the cities, an increasing social complexity, and changing ways of conceptualizing social existence challenged this totalizing view. Dickens's or Collins's London could not be comprehended in the same way as Austen's Bath.

In Collins's novels the narrator cedes authority to the detective (most frequently to the amateur detective who is also a central actor in the mystery whose story is being told). The 'detective' teases out the story that the narrator cannot or will not tell. Facts, events and connections are uncovered or recovered until the knowledge of the reader and the detective(s) coalesces. Far from being the reader's guide and friend, sensation narrators cannot be entirely trusted. They litter our path with false clues, and leave us to make provisional (often wrong) judgements. They allow us temporarily to sympathize with characters and predicaments which both the plot and conventional morality ultimately require us to reject. Thus moral relativism creeps in, at least until the final denouement, and even then it does not always entirely disappear. The reader's sensation of being misled, or temporarily abandoned, by the narrator – of being left free to witness directly the thoughts and actions of unconventional, socially or sexually transgressive or morally dubious characters without the intervention of an all-seeing, all-knowing narrator – is one of the thrills of Collins's sensation novels.

3

The Women's Sensation Novel

> This is the age of the lady novelists, and lady novelists naturally give first place to the heroine[s] . . . [who are] pictured as high-strung women, full of passion, purpose, and movement – very liable to error. Now the most interesting side of a woman's character is her relation to the other sex, and the errors of women that are most interesting spring out of this relation.[1]

Women, above all else, put the sensation (in all its various meanings and forms) into the sensation novel. One of the most sensational things about the sensation genre was the prominence of women writers. For most contemporary commentators this was a fact to be deplored. In *Lucretia: or the Heroine of the Nineteenth Century* (1868) – a satire on the novels of Braddon and Wood – the Reverend Francis E. Paget declared in very strong terms:

> No *man* would have dared to write and publish such books . . . no *man* could have written such delineations of female passion . . . No! They are women, who by their writings have been doing the work of the enemy of souls, glossing over vice, making profligacy attractive, detailing with minuteness the workings of unbridled passions, encouraging vanity, extravagance, wilfulness, selfishness . . . Women have done this, – have thus abused their power and prostituted their gifts, – who might have been bright and shining lights in their generation.

Sensation novels were, in the main (or so it was thought), written by wicked women, about wayward girls and wicked women, for consumption by women whose waywardness and potential for wickedness was signalled by the very fact that they read such material. This unhealthy relationship between women writers, readers and fictional subjects was castigated by Margaret Oliphant, who conducted a one-woman campaign against the genre (although,

40

with her accustomed shrewd professional eye, she also saw that sensationalism played a major part in energizing the rather tame domestic novel, and increasing the market for fiction).

> It is a shame to women so to write; and it is a shame to the women who read and accept as a true representation of themselves and their ways the equivocal talk and fleshly inclinations herein attributed to them. Their patronage of such books is in reality an adoption and acceptance of them.[2]

The predominantly feminine note in sensation fiction was not simply a question of female authorship. The sensation novel was perceived as a feminine phenomenon regardless of the gender of the particular sensation writer. It was yet another symptom of the creeping feminization of literature and culture which began with Richardson and the sentimental novel in the eighteenth century, and became ever more pronounced (and ever more hysterically denounced) as the nineteenth century went on. (For more on this, see Pykett, *The Improper Feminine*, 1992.) It is interesting to note that while the sensation novel was making its stir, writers, readers and critics of poetry were also heatedly debating the issue of the Fleshly School of Poetry. Like the sensation novel, the poems of this school (poems by Dante Gabriel Rossetti, A. C. Swinburne, George Meredith and others) were full of bold and sensual images of 'fallen' and other women, and dealt powerfully with physical sensations. The debate about these poems, like the debate about the sensation novel, turned on issues of gender and ideas about the nature of femininity: the advocates of fleshly poetry declaring that dominant ideas of feminine purity should not be allowed to constrain (masculine) art, and its critics countering that the mode of representation employed (a riot of sensual detail as Alfred Austin put it in an essay on Swinburne in *Temple Bar* in 1869) constituted an (ef-)feminization of art.

The production and consumption of sensation fiction, and its contemporary critical reception were closely linked, not only to general ideas about 'the feminine', but also to various aspects of the Woman Question: to debates about women's legal and political rights, women's educational and employment aspirations and opportunities, and women's dissatisfactions with and resistance to traditional marital and familial patterns. For instance, a review of Braddon's fiction in the *New Review* (1863) explicitly linked the strong, independent sensation heroine to current debates on the position of women:

> When we hear . . . so much about employment for young women, and
> so much scorn cast upon the old-fashioned theory, according to which
> they are intended as help-meets for man . . . are we not driven to ask
> ourselves whether woman's character is of a kind to *bear* emancipation
> from male control and influence?[3]

The recent critical recovery and re-vision of the sensation novel
has also been associated with the Woman Question. The re-reading
of the women's sensation novel has, on the whole, been undertaken
by feminist critics and literary and cultural historians pursuing their
interests in women as writers, readers and written. The women's
sensation novel has been relocated in cultural history by a feminist
scholarship that has re-examined the judgements of traditional
literary history by contextualizing and historicizing the processes of
canon-formation, and by looking more closely at the ways in which
women's writing has been used to construct the boundary between
popular and high art. In particular, feminist critics and cultural
historians have re-examined the evaluative system by means of
which generations of students have been taught 'to equate popularity
with debasement, emotionality with ineffectiveness . . . domesticity
with triviality, and all of these, implicitly, with womanly inferiority'.[4]

Other important new perspectives on the women's sensation novel
have been provided by feminist work on modern mass-culture forms
such as the romantic novel and soap opera. For example, Tania
Modleski's *Loving With a Vengeance* (1984) offers a suggestive analysis
of the semiotics of the popular romance text and the cultural meaning
and significance of genre, discovering 'elements of protest and
resistance underneath highly "orthodox" plots'.[5] Modleski rethinks
the relationships between current 'mass market fantasies for women'
and the women's genres of the past, and analyses them in terms of
the complex and contradictory pleasures which they offer to both
women readers and women writers. Her analysis of gothic and other
women's genres of the eighteenth and early-nineteenth centuries
provides a useful model for re-reading the women's sensation novel
which, like gothic, reworks the conventions and assumptions of
the domestic novel – 'driving home to women the importance of cop-
ing with enforced confinement and the paranoid fear it generates'.[6]

Other feminist work on the texts of modern popular romance has
interrogated the metaphors of passivity, appetite and consumption
which have hitherto dominated thinking about the way in which

women in particular receive the texts of popular culture. Janice Radway's[7] work on Harlequin romance (the American equivalent of Mills and Boon) and its readers has been extremely influential. Radway's combination of ethnographic analysis of actual romance readers and reading communities, with reader-response theory and feminist psychoanalysis produces a view of the activity of romance reading as a deeply contradictory experience. Radway concludes that women readers, paradoxically, appear to immerse themselves in narratives which make an idealized version of domesticity an object of desire, in order to resist and escape, at least temporarily, the limitations of their own domestic and familial roles. Radway's work, like Alison Light's,[8] and Bridget Fowler's,[9] has led to a reassessment of the conventional view that popular romance forms for women depend on the reader's simple identification with the romantic heroine. On the contrary, much of the recent work on mass-market romance tends to suggest that romance texts offer their readers a range of positions and identifications, and that readers quite commonly negotiate those positions and read against the grain of the (frequently) conservative ideology of the formulaic romance text.

The popular texts of the nineteenth century can also be illuminated by using recent work on other modern mass-culture narrative forms; for example, the so-called 'woman's film' (usually a weepy melodrama) and television soap opera. Work on the 'male gaze', on the ways in which the visual text addresses and positions its readers, and the kinds of gendered subjectivity it contructs for them can usefully be appropriated for a re-reading of the women's sensation novel. I have found the feminist intervention in the 'largely negative accounts of female spectatorship, suggesting colonized, alienated or masochistic positions of identification',[10] particularly useful for re-examining what is at issue in the sensation novel's invitation to its female readers to identify with or to spectate women who are victims, subjected to intense suffering or punished for transgressive behaviour. Clearly care is needed; the print culture in which the sensation novel was produced was quite different from the multimedia, mass culture in which radio and television soap opera, the film melodrama and modern mass-market romance fiction have been developed. Nevertheless the study of nineteenth-century literature and culture has much to gain from an engagement with the methodological and theoretical debates within modern cultural studies.

Another source of the renewed interest in the women's sensation novel – and this also overlaps interestingly with the nineteenth-century sensation controversy – is the current interest in writing the feminine and the feminine in writing. Many of the contemporary anxieties about sensation fiction (especially, but not exclusively, as practised by women writers) were expressed as concerns about the 'feminine' nature of the writing. Time and again we see contemporary reviewers complaining that sensation fiction was written in a language of excess: it was extravagant, ornate, embellished; it knew no bounds (or if it did it wilfully ignored them); it dwelt long, lovingly and lavishly on descriptions of the body and of physical sensations – especially, it was objected, when the body or the feelings were those of a woman. Curiously, the reviewers of the middle-class magazines of the sixties were just as concerned with *écriture féminine* and with writing the (female) body as are their late-twentieth-century successors. Needless to say, the disciples of Cixous and Irigary view the matter differently. They seek to appropriate the women's sensation novel as a celebration of female power and feeling, a form of feminine writing which inscribes the body and feminine subjectivity. This is an interesting move, but it risks reinscribing essentialist ideas of the feminine and replicating the gendered critical discourse of the nineteenth century; the main difference is that twentieth-century feminist critics value the 'femininity' which was devalued and marginalized by their nineteenth-century predecessors.

THE SENSATIONAL SPECTACLE OF WOMAN

> There is no good end attained by trying to persuade ourselves that women are all incorporeal, angelic, colourless, passionless, helpless creatures . . . Women have especial need, as the world goes, to be shrewd, self-reliant, and strong; and we do all we can in our literature to render them helpless, imbecilic, and idiotic.[11]

If the sensation novel (and particularly the women's sensation novel) produced a moral panic among the Victorian chattering classes, it was itself produced by another kind of panic – a panic about the nature of the feminine. In the 1860s, woman, womanhood and womanliness all became contested terms, as did the institutions of marriage and the family around which these terms were constructed. The period of the sensation novel's dominance was the decade which immediately followed the agitation leading up to the Divorce Act of

1857 (the Matrimonial Causes Act), the press campaigns on the 'social evil' of prostitution (which also reached a high point in 1857), and the 'surplus women' controversy and the associated campaigns for educational and employment opportunities for women. Throughout the 1860s, in increasingly strident tones, the newspaper and periodical press made a spectacle of 'Woman', put women or 'Woman' on display, and devoted increasing amounts of space to the 'New Woman', the 'fast woman', or, most famously, the 'Girl of the Period'; whatever the label, modern woman was uniformly portrayed as being in flight from motherhood, family responsibility and domestic existence. In these articles, and especially in Eliza Lynn Linton's essay on 'The Girl of the Period' (*Saturday Review*, 14 March 1868), femininity itself was put under the spotlight as an inherently problematic state which involves duplicity, and a potentially uncontrollable feeling; women were represented as primitives, savages, hysterics and whores. The women's sensation novel was part of this developing discourse on the modern woman: it was both a response to and part of social change and a changing conceptualization of women. It also became part of the evidence of these changes.

Above all else, and especially when compared with its immediate predecessor, the domestic novel, the women's sensation novel seems to be concerned with a new sense of marriage and the family as problematic institutions for both women and men. Marriage, the resolution of life's trials and the desired goal of romantic and domestic fiction, is the source of many of life's trials in the sensation novel. The main focus is on the predicament of women, but masculine perspectives on the family, and their troubled experience of romantic love and marriage are also examined in some detail, especially by Braddon and Wood. The novels of the two leading women sensationalists are peopled by frustrated, independent, even mad and murderous women; troubled and troubling wives and mothers; betrayed and betraying husbands, who are either bored or boring, and almost always fail to understand their wives and the domestic sphere in general; strained relations between parents and children, and tensions between siblings.

The sensation novel's preoccupation with marriage questions was frequently articulated in the form of the bigamy plot. Indeed, so common was the female sensationalists' use of this plot that the 'bigamy novel' came to be regarded as a subgenre of the sensation novel. Geraldine Jewsbury, who as a publisher's reader had to wade through all too many manuscripts of derivative bigamy novels, gave vent to her spleen on the genre in a rather illuminating *Athenaeum* review of John Berwick Harwood's *Lord Lynn's Wife*, a novel she had recommended for rejection.

> If, in after-times the manners and customs of English life in 1864 were to be judged from the novels of the day, it would naturally be believed that people, in the best regulated families, were in the habit of marrying two wives, or two husbands . . . and of suppressing the one that proved inconvenient, either by 'painless extinction' or by more forcible methods.[12]

Of course, this is a salutary warning on the use of literary 'evidence', but the novels of 1864 do, in fact, give the reader of after-times much valuable evidence about the concerns and anxieties, if not the practices of the majority of the best-regulated families of the Victorian bourgeoisie. Jewsbury also offers a perceptive analysis of the socio-legal origins and psychological appeal of the bigamy plot.

> Heroes and heroines of the present generation of novels rarely dispense with the marriage ceremony altogether, – it would be a want of propriety which would shock both author and reader; but illegal marriage and supernumerary ceremonies are the order of the day . . . [and] we must conclude that there is a great deal of latent sympathy with this state of things, which an author can appeal to with the certainty of exciting the reader's lively interest.[13]

Bigamy in the sensation novel is usually accidental or inadvertent, that is to say it involves a marriage which both of the partners believe to be valid, but which is not – usually because of some legal oddity or the erroneous belief that the first husband or wife is dead. This kind of bigamy plot had a powerful psychological appeal, and was a useful narrative device in the respectable middle-class novel (and this for all its flirtations with the risqué, is what the sensation novel remained). Such plots involve moral complexity as well as narrative complication. As Jeanne Fahnestock has pointed out (in an excellent essay on the subject) inadvertent or unintentional bigamy plots 'allow their protagonists to be paradoxically both innocent and guilty at the same time'.[14] They offer the chance 'to sin and be innocent . . . to see unsocial desires fulfilled and duly punished'. These plots also allow readers to identify with a sexually transgressive and guilty character, and vicariously to experience a guilt from which they are sub-sequently released – a very satisfying process.

French novels have adultery; the English, more concerned with propriety and the blush on the cheek of the young person, stick to bigamy. True, on the whole. But, of course, one must remember the interesting exception. *East Lynne*, written by the conservative Ellen Wood, and one of the most popular novels of the nineteenth century, is a novel whose nobly suffering heroine is incontrovertibly an adulteress. However, even in this case (perhaps, as we shall see later, especially in this case), the bigamy convention is kept in play. Although Carlyle, the 'betrayed' husband, does not remarry until he has good reason to believe his wife is dead, he nevertheless suspects himself a bigamist when he discovers that the governess employed by his new wife is his first (divorced) wife in disguise: 'the first thought that came thumping through his brain was, that he must be man of two wives'. Carlyle's reaction dramatizes a new moral experience created by the reformed divorce laws: a tension between marriage merely as a socio-legal arrangement, and moral and religious conceptions of marriage.

Some sensation novelists developed what one might call spiritual or imagined bigamy or adultery plots, in which heroines are legally married to one man while feeling themselves to be spiritually or emotionally married to another, or, alternatively, in which single heroines feel themselves to be bound to unattainable or married men. Rhoda Broughton's *Cometh Up as a Flower* and *Not Wisely But Too Well* are examples of this species of what Oliphant described as 'innocent indecency'.[15] *Cometh Up as a Flower*, a particularly interesting reworking of some important sensation themes, portrays a 'free-spoken heroine'[16] who marries a rich, older man for prudential reasons and from a sense of familial obligation, although she is passionately in love with a handsome young soldier called Dick. This plot allows Broughton to indulge her readers in numerous scenes depicting the feverish imagining of her heroine, or moments of illicit passion. Broughton also uses this situation to give a deeply felt representation of the horrors of a prudential loveless marriage. Readers such as Oliphant found the narrator-heroine's clear-eyed view of the nature of her marital situation, and the frank tones in which she described it, particularly shocking. Others might have found it too near the mark for comfort when the heroine describes her marriage as, 'the most matter of fact piece of barter in the world;

so much young flesh for so much current coin of the realm' (*CUF* 315), or when she narrates her sensations of repulsion at her husband's touch:

> His arm is around my waist and he is brushing my eyes and cheeks . . . with his somewhat bristly moustache as often as he feels inclined – for am I not his property . . . for has he not bought me . . . for so many pounds of prime white flesh, he has paid down handsomely on the nail . . . that accursed, girdling arm is still round me – my buyer's arm – that arm which seems to be burning into my flesh like a brand. (*CUF* 325)

This sense of marriage as a form of prostitution would be taken up by the women novelists of the 1880s and 1890s.

An adulterous or bigamous marriage would, of course, be a fairly substantial skeleton to have in the family cupboard. As we saw in the previous chapter, family secrets, and fundamental fears about the nature and structure of the family were central to all of Collins's novels of the sensational sixties. Such fearful secrets were even more important in the women's sensation novel. Indeed Elaine Showalter, writing mainly on the female sensationalists, has gone so far as to suggest that 'the power of Victorian sensation derives . . . from its exposure of secrecy as the fundamental and enabling condition of middle-class life.[17] The sensationalists' obsession with family secrets was much remarked upon by their first readers. In 'Sensation Novelists: Miss Braddon', W. Fraser Rae protested that novelists like Braddon:

> want to persuade people that in almost every one of the well-ordered houses of their neighbours there was a skeleton shut up in some cupboard; that their comfortable and easy-looking neighbour had in his breast a secret story which he was always going about trying to conceal.[18]

This persuasion is by no means a concealed subtext of the women's sensation novel; it is very much part of the textual surface. Characters speculate about 'the mysteries that may hang about the houses we enter' and 'foul deeds . . . done under the most hospitable roofs (*LAS* 140). The omniscient narrators of Braddon and Wood opine that 'few of us are without some secret skeleton that we have to keep . . . from the world' (Wood, *Lord Oakburn's Daughters*, 339), and openly and portentously alert the reader to family secrets, spectres from the past, and the horrors that lurk beneath domestic calm and apparent rural tranquillity. Here is a well-known and, I like to think, tongue-in-cheek, example from *Lady Audley's Secret*.

We hear every day of murder committed in the country. Brutal and treacherous murders; slow, protracted agonies from poisons administered by some *kindred* hand; sudden and violent deaths by cruel blows, inflicted with a stake cut from some spreading oak, whose very shadow promised – peace. In the county of which I write, I have been shown a meadow in which, on a quiet summer Sunday evening, a young farmer murdered the girl who had loved and trusted him; and yet even now . . . the aspect of the spot is – peace. (*LAS* 54, my emphasis)

In the women's sensation novel (as in Collins's) the emphasis is very much on domestic violence and domestic crime: poisoning by a 'kindred' hand, crimes of passion, and intra-familial rivalries which lead to conspiracies to do with wills and the ownership of property. The women sensationalists have their fair share of male criminals – fraudsters, kidnappers, blackmailers, and even murderers – but their most remarkable and remarked-upon criminals and wrong-doers are women: Braddon's Lady Audley, the murderous bigamist; the tempestuous Aurora Floyd, a bigamist with a tendency to horsewhip her servants; Olivia Arundel (in *John Marchmont's Legacy*), who engages in a conspiracy to kidnap the wife of the man she loves; and Wood's Lady Isabel Vane, who, although not technically a criminal, is in effect guilty of crimes against womanhood and the family.

It seems to me, however, that the most striking thing about the women writers' sensation heroine is not her criminality; it is her deviance and transgressiveness. The sensation heroine's failure to conform to social codes is even more significant, and potentially more subversive, than her breaking of laws. Similarly, the most striking thing about the manner in which she is represented is the way in which that representation subverts, questions, or otherwise complicates, dominant ideas and images of 'Woman'. The central female characters of the women's sensation novel are of two main types: active, assertive women, who convey a sense of the threat of insurgent femininity trying to break out of the doll's house of domesticity, and passive, dependent women, who are imprisoned by it, unable to articulate their sense of confinement, and driven to desperate measures.

Braddon and Wood, in particular, unsettle conventional images of woman by investing sympathy in, and attaching unexpected moral valuations to, particular character stereotypes. Thus the woman who looks and (ostensibly) acts like the angel in the house turns out to be a demon in the house, who commits crimes in order to obtain socially sanctioned goals such as a good marriage. The fallen woman (who in terms of the dominant code of representation can only be portrayed as a prostitute, and thus as completely beyond the moral pale) is, on occasions, represented as more pure than the socially accepted woman who stays carefully (and, sometimes, cynically) within the bounds of convention. The heroine who conforms most closely to the feminine ideal is not idealized; she is portrayed as a victim, and the childlike innocence and clinging dependence which constitute the domestic feminine ideal are exposed as the sources of her victimhood. The women sensationalists thus engage in a complex process of negotiating, and, in the end, of revising and rewriting, that feminine tradition of submission and renunciation which was a powerful fact of both literature and life.

Nowhere is this negotiation of conventional images of femininity more apparent than in the women sensationalists' representation of motherhood. Maternity is in a sense the key to the representation of femininity in virtually all forms of Victorian discourse. The ideological constructs of femininity, womanhood and womanliness were all defined through the maternal function of biological females. The dominant characteristics of this version of femininity, from hysteria to spiritual refinement, from a potentially engulfing sexuality to self-sacrificing affectivity, were 'deemed equally the products of the uterine economy'.[19] Motherhood is the constant subtext of the women's sensation novel: absent (dead) mothers, neglectful mothers, abandoning mothers, over-invested mothers who neglect their husbands, mothers who spoil their children with an excess of indulgent love (often with disastrous consequences, when that child is a son), mothers who are also murderers (unthinkably to middle-class ideologues, despite the examples of history and of classical tragedy). As we shall see, the treatment of motherhood in the women's sensation novel is the source of various and complex narrative satisfactions for the reader, especially the woman reader.

Along with the mother, the motherless girl is the most important figure in the women's sensation novel, as Margaret Oliphant noted: 'Ill-brought-up motherless girls, left to grow anyhow, out of all feminine guardianship, have become the ideal of the novelist'.[20] The lack of a mother renders the sensation heroine both more assertive and independent and/or more vulnerable than the woman who has been conventionally socialized under the surveillance and guidance of a mother. Aurora Floyd's wildness, for example, is attributed to the lack of that careful mothering required to 'train and prune' the 'exuberant branches' which develop in women in their natural state, and which must be 'trimmed and clipped and fastened primly to the stone wall of society with cruel nails' (*AF* 42). As Braddon's horticultural metaphor suggests, the women sensationalists are much preoccupied with the relationship between woman in her 'natural' state and the socialized forms of femininity.

MARY ELIZABETH BRADDON

Mary Elizabeth Braddon was widely acknowledged as the un-crowned queen of the sensation novel, who, as a writer in the *North British Review* put it in 1865, was possessed of a power to bewitch the 'unthinking crowd' (vol. 43, p. 180). Braddon was well prepared for this role by her earlier careers as actress and hack writer for the penny dreadfuls. She took to the stage at 22 to help support her mother who had been deserted by Braddon's father. By 1860 she was established in London, furiously penning pulp for the magazines, a practice she kept up even after her success as a sensationalist. Braddon wrote constantly in order to earn enough money to support herself, her partner (the publisher John Maxwell), their five illegitimate children, and the children of his legal marriage (his wife, in an uncanny echo of the sensation plot, was an inmate of a Dublin lunatic asylum).

Clearly Braddon's knowledge of the melodramatic repertoire provided her with fictional subjects and situations, and some of the effects of her practical experience of staging can be seen in the style and structure of her sensation novels, not least in her frequent use of dramatic tableaux. The unconventional life of an actress also exposed her to an experience much wider and freer than that available to the average middle-class girl growing up in the drawing-room under the strict surveillance of the maternal eye. As Henry James pointed out in his appreciative review of Braddon's novels, 'she knows much that ladies are not accustomed to know, but that they are apparently very glad to learn'.[21] Similarly, Braddon's apprenticeship on the penny dreadfuls gave her a facility for recycling other people's plots and developing endless variations on the same themes. As she explained to Bulwer Lytton (who had developed his own brand of sensationalism in the 1830s), 'the amount of crime, treachery, murder, slow poisoning, and general infamy required by the halfpenny reader is something terrible'.[22]

Braddon, like Ellen Wood, 'Ouida' and Rhoda Broughton, enjoyed a long career as a writer (her last novel was published in 1886). She produced *seventeen* novels in the 1860s, over half of which could be described as sensation novels, and she went on to produce another seventeen novels in the 1870s, mostly social satires and novels of manners. In fact Braddon was always a satirist. Much of her originality and force as a sensationalist came from her witty mockery of social and literary modes. Braddon rarely simply repeated the formulas of the sensation novel; she was engaged in a constant process of negotiation and revision of its conventions. She parodied and satirized sensationalism, and she was a commentator on the genre's power and foibles – in her letters to Bulwer Lytton and through her mouthpiece Sigismund Smith, a sensation novelist who first appears in *The Doctor's Wife* and who reappears in several different incarnations in later novels.

THE HISTORIES OF IMPERFECT WOMEN

> if she had been faultless she could not have been the heroine of this story; for has not some wise old man of old remarked, that the perfect women are those who leave no histories behind them. (*AF* 330)

Braddon's narratives (like most sensation novels) have their origins in female inperfection. Braddon's heroines are, for one reason or another, not what they seem. Most of her sensation narratives are structured around women with something to hide, some secret in the past which makes their present life a sham or masquerade. In those novels which are less well known to modern readers (because out of print), that secret is often a family secret connected with the heroine's father. The father in these novels is, at best, weak, vain, neglectful of his family responsibilities and exploitative of his daughter. At worst, he is a criminal. Because his guilt both compromises the heroine's social respectability and produces in her a sense of guilt by association, she tends to conceal his true nature from herself and/or to conceal his existence from the world. The plots of these novels (for example, *Eleanor's Victory, Run To Earth,*

Henry Dunbar, The Doctor's Wife) are constructed around the complexities and contradictions of women's conflicting familial roles as daughters, wives and mothers.

In Braddon's most powerful novels, the secrets which drive the narrative are those of the heroine's own criminal past, or those of her own dark and demonic depths. These novels include Braddon's two most famous successes, *Lady Audley's Secret* and *Aurora Floyd*, and also the long out-of-print *John Marchmont's Legacy*, which contains, in Olivia Arundel, one of the most remarkable representations of a daughter of the vicarage to be found in Victorian fiction. *Lady Audley's Secret*, Braddon's mischievous reworking of *The Woman in White*, was greeted as 'one of the most noxious books of modern times'[23] because of its portrayal of the sweetly smiling, golden haired Lucy Graham (later Audley), who was 'at once the heroine and the monstrosity of the novel',[24] a Lady Macbeth in the shape of the feminine ideal; 'the lovely woman with the fishy extremities' ('Lady Audley's Secret', *The Times*, 18 November 1862, p. 8).

> Wherever she went she seemed to take joy and brightness with her. In the cottages of the poor her fair face shone like a sunbeam . . . [she] was blessed with that magic power of fascination by which a woman can charm with a word or intoxicate with a smile. Every one loved, admired, and praised her. (*LAS* 5–6)

Lucy Graham is certainly not what she seems, but she plays the part of the submissive, complaisant, feminine ideal so well that she captivates a foolish old baronet, and almost everyone in sight. Female 'fascination' and the power of the myth of the feminine ideal sustain Lucy's masquerade for much of the novel. The reader too is fascinated, but also disturbed. The representation of Lady Audley is a bold assault on the reader's preconceptions about women in both literature and life. It satirizes the feminine ideal by exaggerating its contours, but it also dramatizes numerous anxieties about that ideal and about the female forces which it is designed to keep in check. *Lady Audley's Secret* pleases, thrills, shocks and undermines its readers with the fact that this personification of simpering, charitable, childlike, genteel femininity is, in fact, a cold, calculating, resourceful woman, who abandons her child and is capable of murder, all in the interests of self-preservation. The irony is that all of Lucy's actions are aimed at those ends which were recommended to all middle-class girls: achieving and maintaining a socially acceptable and financially secure marriage, and keeping up appearances.

Braddon represents Lucy as an actress and a chameleon, and thus plays on the reader's fears and fantasies about the duplicity of women. Before the action of the novel begins, Lucy (as Helen Maldon), the daughter of a disreputable half-pay naval officer, has made what she thinks is a socially advantageous marriage, only to discover that her outraged father-in-law has disinherited her husband, who promptly leaves to seek his fortunes in Australia (a continent of immense usefulness to Victorian novelists in need of a convenient black hole in which to make characters disappear). Lucy (now Helen Talboys) does not go into a decline to await rescue by some shining knight, nor does she fall onto the streets (as she might if she 'really' were the vulnerable, childlike woman she appears). Instead, she carefully stages her own death (complete with *Times* obituary notice), and reinvents herself as Lucy Graham, writes herself some references and obtains a post as a governess, leaving her infant son with her father.

Is she mad, or is she just bad? The novel (deliberately?) blurs the issue. Viewed from one end of the telescope of Victorian ideology, Helen/Lucy's histrionics are but another version of that hysteria to which all women are prone (the product of her puerperal fever perhaps, or insanity inherited from her mother). Viewed from the other end of the telescope, Helen/Lucy's role-playing is a particularly acute form of Victorian self-fashioning:

> I had learnt that which in some indefinite manner or other *every schoolgirl learns sooner or later* – I learned that my ultimate fate in life depended upon my marriage, and I concluded that if I was indeed prettier than my schoolfellows, I ought to marry better than any of them. (*LAS* 350, my emphasis)

A girl has to do what a girl has to do, when marriage is the most secure career choice open to the genteel woman. What is shocking is that Lucy not only does it, she *says* it.

If the feminine ideal is an illusion, even a fraud, what then is conventional marriage, which is produced by and which reproduces that ideal? This novel provides some discomforting answers in its representation of a marriage built on a tissue of lies, impersonation, fraud and murder. As in Collins's sensation novels, the detection of this dreadful secret is mainly the work of a man who polices the family; in this case the family policeman is Robert Audley, Sir Michael's nephew. Robert is a familiar type in the sensation novel; a type produced by the genre's preoccupation with the construction of gendered identities, and by its complex juxtapositioning of aristocratic and bourgeois value. Robert, like Hartright and Franklin Blake, begins the novel as a liminal figure who lacks a masculine identity and vocation. He is supposedly reading for the Bar, but is actually spending his time in a state of feminized, aristocratic indolence, reading French novels (always a dangerous sign in Victorian fiction). As in Collins's novels, the route to masculinity is the discovery of the secrets of the family, and the simultaneous discovery of a vocation and a commitment to the work ethic. For Robert the family becomes his work. In his efforts to solve the mystery of his friend George Talboys's 'dead' wife, and to penetrate the secrets of Lady Audley, Robert develops those legal skills (assembling documents and marshalling a logical case) which he had merely found tedious before he discovered a motive for his existence. The motive force for Robert's journey to a properly socialized bourgeois masculinity is woman, or rather, two women: the 'fascinating' and bewitching Lady Audley, who merely impersonates the feminine ideal, and Clara Talboys (George's sister), who actually is the feminine ideal. Robert's discovery of Clara begins the process by which he reconstructs his own feminized identity, represses his own attraction to Lady Audley's dangerous femininity, and expels it from the family.

In one of Braddon's most interesting reworkings of the plot of *The Woman in White*, she has her hero re-enact the role that Collins gave to his villain. In Collins's novel the hero rescues victimized women from lunatic asylums, to which they have been consigned by a villain who wants to gain control of their wealth or prevent them from telling his secrets. In Braddon's novel the hero plots to have a woman incarcerated in a lunatic asylum, to prevent her from telling her own secrets. Having exposed his aunt's secrets, Robert must repress them. His newly discovered masculinity and commitment to the family is constructed upon a version of femininity which cannot contain that other version of femininity represented by Lucy; it can contain the madwoman, but not the murderess.

Containing femininity is what the end of this novel is all about. Robert's discussions with doctors expose the way in which madness was used by the Victorian medical profession as a convenient way of labelling and managing disruptive femininity. As the medical expert called in by Robert puts it: 'The lady is not mad . . . She has the cunning of madness, with the prudence of intelligence. I will tell you what she is . . . She is dangerous! (*LAS* 379). Braddon also uses madness as a way of figuring dangerous femininity in her portrayal of Olivia Arundel in *John Marchmont's Legacy*. Whereas Lucy Audley's mask of the passionless woman of the feminine ideal conceals cold, prudential calculation, Olivia's conventional (even conventual) appearance and her role as the dutiful daughter of the vicarage mask a darkly passionate nature. Lady Audley's story ends with her containment in a lunatic asylum modelled on the bourgeois household in order that the middle-class family and the feminine ideal on which it is constructed may be defended from the threat she presents. Olivia, on the other hand, is represented as the prisoner of that ideal. If *Lady Audley's Secret* raises the question of whether madness is simply a label that is attached to deviant femininity, *John Marchmont's Legacy* raises the even more interesting question of whether madness is a *symptom* of bourgeois femininity.

Olivia Arundel cherishes a passionate and secret love for her cousin Edward, but she has an even better kept secret – 'the bitter discontent grown fierce and mad' (as Carlyle wrote of the working classes in 'Chartism' in 1839) of her 'fearfully monotonous, narrow and uneventful life' (*JML* vol. 1, p. 134). Olivia is a fascinating portrait of female repression, living her life within a 'narrow boundary':

> performing and repeating the same duties from day to day, with no other progress to mark the lapse of her existence than the slow alternation of the seasons, and the dark hollow circles which had lately deepened beneath her grey eyes . . . These outward tokens, beyond her control, alone betrayed this woman's secret. She was weary of her life. She sickened under [its] dull burden . . . The slow round of duty was loathsome to her. The horrible, narrow, unchanging existence, shut in by cruel walls which bounded her in on every side and kept her prisoner to herself, was odious to her. The powerful intellect revolted against the fetters that bound and galled it. The proud heart beat with murderous violence against the bonds that kept it captive. (*JML* vol. 1, pp. 135–6)

This is powerful stuff by any standards, and likely to produce a complex response of recognition and rebuttal in the contemporary female reader. Of course, in the end, we are meant to reject Olivia, who is driven to plotting and crime by her thwarted nature and her frustrated love for Edward. Before we do, however, we have more than a pang of sympathy for this wasted life, confined by the iron chains of convention.

The lengthy passage quoted above is evidence of Braddon's self-professed admiration for the 'Balzac morbid anatomy school' (letter to Edmund Yates).[25] It is also typical of the melodramatic excess of her own sensation style. Braddon habitually uses this style in the set-piece scenes and dramatic tableaux which display her main female characters as a spectacle to the reader's gaze. The reader is repeatedly invited to look at the central female character, or to look at the narrator or the other characters looking at her. Perhaps the most famous example of this specularity is in Braddon's use of the Pre-Raphaelite portrait of Lady Audley which I discuss in some detail elsewhere.[26]

Contemporary reviewers complained about the sensuality and sexual depravity of Braddon's heroines. I think that Braddon's first readers were making an interesting displacement here. In actual fact Braddon's women seem remarkably uninterested in sex, especially when they are compared with Rhoda Broughton's heroines, who exist in a permanent state of throbbing palpitation, before going into a decline, worn out with unconsummated passion. On the whole, Braddon's women are presented not as desiring, sexual subjects, but as sexual objects. This, I think, is an effect of the regime of looking, and of the dominant codes for representing the female body in nineteenth-century writing and painting (see H. Michie, *The Flesh Made Word*, 1987). Time and again Braddon's novels represent their female characters through their physical appearance, especially their hair (Victorian reviewers made much of this fetishism). Olivia Arundel's hair is both sign and symptom of her failure to conform to the feminine ideal:

> Those masses of hair had not that purple lustre, nor yet that wandering glimmer of red gold, which gives peculiar beauty to some raven tresses. Olivia's hair was long and luxuriant; but it was of that dead, inky blackness, which is all shadow. It was dark, fathomless, inscrutable, like herself. (*JML* vol. 1, p. 141)

The impetuous, inadvertent-bigamist heroine of *Aurora Floyd* is the object of a similar treatment. In Aurora's case the mode of representation is doubly voyeuristic, since the reader is usually invited to watch someone watching Aurora. The heroine is first seen through the eyes of Talbot Bulstrode, her first suitor, who rejects her when he hears rumours of her youthful escapades in Paris. To Bulstrode, who is muscular manliness personified (complete with aristocratic pedigree and a closed mind on the woman question), Aurora appears as 'A divinity! imperiously beautiful in white and scarlet, painfully dazzling to look upon, intoxicatingly brilliant to behold' (*AF* 29). The gap between masculine fantasies of divine womanhood and the untidy realities of actual women is brought home sharply by the words uttered by this apparition: 'Do you know if Thunderbolt won the Leger?'

This voyeuristic form of representation is used, in part, to explore different ways of perceiving femininity. The differing perceptions of Talbot Bulstrode and John Mellish are interestingly juxtaposed, particularly their perceptions of the striking, impetuous, racy, 'Girl of the Period' Aurora and her blonde cousin Lucy, the somewhat insipid personification of the feminine ideal. The voyeuristic method is also used as a means of controlling the reader's response to Aurora, and to the version of femininity she represents. Thus at the crux of the narrative, when the unravelling of Aurora's 'miserable secrets' has brought her to 'the threshold of darker miseries', the reader is invited to join John Mellish in watching the unwitting heroine as she sleeps.

> Aurora was lying on the sofa, wrapped in a loose white dressing-gown, her masses of ebon hair uncoiled and falling about her shoulders in serpentine tresses that looked like shining blue-black snakes released from poor Medusa's head to make their escape amid the folds of her garment. (*AF* 227)

This Pre-Raphaelite word-painting pictures Aurora as an object of erotic desire and, at the same time, a non-threatening, self-contained, almost auto-erotic creature (the snakes, for example, are burying themselves in her clothes, not directed outwards to the spectator). Readers, male and female alike, are thus offered a pleasurable image of erotic power, but the potential danger of this female erotic power is defused and contained by framing, just as Aurora herself is eventually framed by the family and contained by motherhood.

Aurora is, in the end, rescued for womanhood by an ordeal of suffering and by maternity. First, Aurora's disruptive femininity is contained by the threatened loss of her home and husband, and she is brought within the boundaries of the womanly behaviour, she has hitherto despised and refused. During this process the reader is positioned as the spectator of Aurora's drama of suffering, and is the recipient of the narrator's woman-to-woman address on the heroine's predicament.

> Ah, careless wives! who think it a small thing, perhaps, that your husbands are honest and generous, constant and true, and who are apt to grumble because your . . . neighbours have started a carriage . . . stop and think of this wretched girl, who in this hour of desolation recalled a thousand little wrongs she had done to her husband, and would have laid herself under his feet to be walked over by him could she have thus atoned for her petty tyrannies . . . Think of her in her loneliness, with her heart yearning to go back to the man she loved. (*AF* 290)

The rhetoric of this passage works to reinforce conventional womanly virtues by directly addressing both the reader's possible marital discontents and her guilt at her own womanly failings. By allowing the reader to identify with a socially and sexually transgressive woman, it also allows her to experience vicariously the frisson of having lost the benefits of the love of an honest and good man – benefits which, by implication, are undervalued by the conventional bourgeois wife. Although this novel speaks with several voices on the marriage question (the conventionally ideal marriage of Talbot Bulstrode and the fair Lucy comes in for some particularly good understated satire), the effect of this passage is to 'talk up' the value of ordinary marriage.

The second step in Aurora's redemption for womanliness is her embracing of the maternal role. *Aurora Floyd* thus offers a challenging and exciting, even seductive image of the 'Girl of the Period' before putting her back in place – albeit with a touch of parody – as the repentant wife and doating mother: 'a little changed, a shade less defiantly bright, but unspeakably beautiful and tender, bending over the cradle of her first-born' (*AF* 384). Aurora (and the woman reader) is, in this novel, if not in life, allowed to have it all (although not all at once): a racy, adventurous youth followed by marriage to an adoring man, and doating motherhood.

ELLEN WOOD

> It is not pleasant to write of these things . . . but I know of few histories
> where they can be entirely avoided, if the whole truth has to be adhered
> to, for many and evil are the passions that assail the undisciplined human
> heart. (*Verner's Pride*, 208)

'Pleasant' or not, the passions of the undisciplined human heart, and
the processes by which women and men learn to govern them, or –
more interestingly – succumb to them, provide the sensational
material of Ellen Wood's otherwise sentimental novels. A bald
summary of the core of the plot of *East Lynne* might make it appear
to be the most outrageous of the sensation novels of the early sixties.
Its heroine, Lady Isabel Carlyle (née Vane), is a beautiful and refined
young woman, who deserts her decent, hard-working husband and
infant children, and elopes with an aristocratic seducer, whose
illegitimate child she bears after he has deserted her. So far, so
shocking; but the wages of all this sinning turn out, after all
(reassuringly), to be death. The erring heroine is made an example
to would-be errant wives.

Despite her errant behaviour Isabel remains the heroine; she is
represented as a sinner rather than a villain or criminal, and she
retains the readers' sympathies to the end. Indeed, sympathy for
Isabel's sufferings and the complexities of her predicament increases
as her social and moral standing declines. *East Lynne*, like Wood's
other novels of the 1860s, is, as Winifred Hughes has asserted, an
example of the sensation novel as 'pure soap opera, loaded down
with pathos, disaster, tortures of guilt and repentance'.[27] However,
like modern film or television soap opera, it offers a complex range
of messages, meanings and satisfactions to its audience. *East Lynne*
is not the straightforwardly simple tale of pious, conventional
morality that it appears at first sight.

It is easy to understand why some early reviewers of the novel
should have seen Wood's novel as an example of the sensation
genre's obsession with women bent on doing as they like, and loving
whom they like. *East Lynne* is, after all, the story of an adulteress.
However, when this novel dwells on the sensations of its heroine, it
dwells less on her sensual longings for male muscles, and more on
her frustrated maternal feelings. Isabel's adultery is, in a sense, but
a means to an end; its main narrative function is to produce the
circumstances which give rise to that 'prolonged and luxurious orgy

of self-torture'[28] which constitutes the most powerful part of the novel.

East Lynne is, pre-eminently, the story of a mother, and of a mother's sufferings. This is still a powerfully appealing theme to women readers, and for much the same reasons as in the 1860s, when motherhood and womanhood, and the links between the two, were being hotly contested. One of the most important contrasts in the novel is that between the two wives of Archibald Carlyle: the aristocratic Isabel Vane, who gives way to feeling, suffers and dies, and the bourgeois Barbara Hare, who endures jealousy, learns to control feeling, and survives. The most important point of contrast between Isabel and Barbara is their differing responses to motherhood. The second Mrs Carlyle (Barbara) is a rational, modern mother. Her conduct as a wife and mother, and her views on these roles seem to come straight out of the conduct books, those advice manuals with which nineteenth-century women were inundated.[29] Thus, in a moment of exquisitely poignant irony, the second Mrs Carlyle addresses the first Mrs Carlyle (now disguised as governess to her own children) on the subject of family management:

> I hold an opinion . . . that too many mothers pursue a mistaken system in the management of their family. There are some, we know, who lost in the pleasures of the world, in frivolity, wholly neglect them . . . nothing can be more thoughtless . . . but there are others who err on the opposite side. They are never happy but when with their children. They wash them, dress them, feed them . . . [such a mother] loses her authority . . . The discipline of that house soon becomes broken. The children run wild; the husband is sick of it, and seeks peace and solace elsewhere . . . I shall never give up to another . . . the training of my children . . . This is a mother's task. (*EL* 415–16)

Mrs Sarah Ellis, whose books on the conduct of the wives, daughters and mothers of England were extremely influential, put the matter more succinctly:

> wherever a mother thus doats upon her children, she is guilty of an act of unfaithfulness to her husband, at the same time that she places herself in a perilous position, from whence the first shock of disease, or the first symptom of ingratitude, may cast her down into utter wretchedness.[30]

Isabel is an example of the doating mother, whose first act of unfaithfulness to her husband (with her children) is quickly followed by the utter wretchedness of her actual adultery with Levison.

However, the contrast between the two Mrs Carlyles is not a simple one. Even as Barbara is mouthing the conduct book moralisms which are the source of her survival – moralisms with which many of Wood's readers would have agreed – those same readers are being positioned so as to identify and sympathize with the sufferings of Isabel the over-invested or doating mother. Morally the reader is asked to approve of Barbara's bourgeois prudence, which 'proves' itself more serviceable by winning the day. Emotionally, however, the reader is allowed to enjoy and value the feelings of and for Isabel, feelings of aristocratic excess, which must in the end be rejected. This fracturing of the reader's response replicates the contradictions in mid-Victorian ideologies of motherhood and womanhood.

Woman, as constructed in Victorian ideology, is asexual and passionless, and yet she is the repository of feeling and the source of affectivity. This contradiction is held together by the notion of domestic woman, of whom William Acton wrote, 'love of home, children, and domestic duties, are the only passions they feel'.[31] In moral discourse, woman is all spirit (and hence disembodied), and yet in medical discourse she is all body, a body in thrall to its reproductive function. Femininity is defined in terms of renunciation and submission, but these have different meanings when applied to the mother as opposed to the wife: the woman-as-mother sacrifices all for the reproduction of the race; the woman-as-wife sacrifices all for the well-being of the husband. The doctrine of renunciation and submission also leads to moral contradictions, to models of moral conduct which are differently gendered, and to a potential moral enfeeblement of women. John Stuart Mill pointed out some of these problems in *The Subjection of Woman* (1869).

> All the moralities tell women that it is their duty, and all the current sentimentalities, that it is their nature to live for others; to make complete abnegations of themselves, and to have no life but in their affections. (p. 27)

These are some of the conflicts and contradictions from which the drama of *East Lynne* is constructed. They are unified by one thing: the need to control, regulate and manage that feminine feeling that women were taught that they were unable to control for themselves. Their 'ideal of character', wrote Mill, 'is the very opposite of that of men; not self-will, and government by self-control, but submission, and yielding to the control of others' (p. 27).

Wood's novel manages these contradictions by her own particular combination of sin and sentiment, which involves reworking the conventions of domestic fiction as sensationalized domestic melodrama. Braddon's *Lady Audley's Secret* and *Aurora Floyd* eroticize the female body, and make a spectacle of the racy, assertive woman, or the calculating dangerous woman in domestic disguise. *East Lynne*, on the other hand, eroticizes feminine (womanly) feeling, and makes a spectacle of the sufferings of the female victim. In particular it makes a spectacle of maternal suffering. In this novel the absent mother is seen, not from the point of view of the (female) child's lack of nurture, but from the point of view of the needy mother. Maternal deprivation is at the centre of this maternal melodrama. This term, which is more usually applied to film than to novels, is perhaps one of the most useful generic terms to apply to *East Lynne*, and suggests interesting ways of reading Wood's text. Maternal melodrama is a form which primarily addresses female audiences about issues which mainly concern women. It habitually places its audience within a range of feminine subject positions, and demands the particular 'reading competence' associated with the specific form of feminine subjectivity produced by 'the social fact of female mothering'.[32] In *East Lynne* this positioning is effected by presenting events from Isabel's point of view, or by the very simple device of the gossipy tone with which the narrator engages the (putative) female reader in a direct woman-to-woman address.

Apart from motherhood, domestic life is one of the women's issues which *East Lynne* directly addresses, mainly (although not exclusively) from a woman's point of view. The novel offers two sharply juxtaposed images of the domestic power which was ceded to women by the ideology of the separate spheres: the tyrannical, shrewish old maid, Cornelia (Carlyle's half-sister), and the epitome of modern domestic competence, Barbara Hare/Carlyle. But, once more, the most powerful representations of domestic existence are those which focus on Isabel's predicament: first as the misunderstood and tormented orphan in her aunt's household; then as the wife who is misunderstood by a husband who is preoccupied with his career, and apparently incapable of seeing his wife's isolation and her exclusion from the running of the household by his officious half-sister. (The novel seems to suggest that Carlyle's incomprehension is structural; it is a function of the male position within the feminine sphere of the home.) Finally the narrative focuses on Isabel, in her disguise of governess, as the outsider who watches her erstwhile family carrying on with their lives (and deaths) having erased her from the family record. In all of these circumstances Isabel is represented as confined, entrapped, persecuted and suffering within the very space, the home, which was supposedly the sanctuary of women.

Wood's depiction of women's domestic entrapment and subordination directly addresses the actual or potential dissatisfactions of women readers. However, it also works to contain and manage those dissatisfactions. No matter how frustrating, hostile or uncomfortable, the family and the domestic sphere are represented as essential both for the protection of women, and for the containment of feminine excess. Isabel is most endangered and most dangerous when she is exiled – against her own wishes – for the purposes of convalescence in France. Removed from the protective bosom of her family she is extremely vulnerable to Levison's seductive offensive, and hence becomes a threat to the stability of a society which is based on the control of women's sexuality.

One of the novel's most important devices for managing women's domestic discontents is the prolonged 'orgy of self-torture' mentioned earlier. In the final volume Isabel is persistently represented as the pained and longing spectator of the family she had wilfully deserted, and the witness of scenes of domestic intimacy between the husband she now loves and his new wife. Instead of being the cause of discontent, the family thus becomes for Isabel, as it does for the reader, the object of desire. The narrator's voice also works to reposition its female readers as domestic creatures. One example must suffice, but the novel is full of passages such as this one which records Isabel's awakening conscience:

> Oh, reader, believe me! Lady – wife – mother! should you ever be tempted to abandon your home, so will you awake. Whatever trials may be the lot of your married life, though they may magnify themselves to your crushed spirit as beyond the endurance of woman to bear, *resolve* to bear them; fall down upon your knees and pray to be enabled to bear them . . . bear unto death, rather than forfeit your fair name and your good conscience; for be assured that the alternative if you rush on to it, will be found far worse than death.
>
> Poor . . . Lady Isabel! She had sacrificed husband, children, reputation, home, all that makes life of value to woman. (*EL* 289)

This address to the reader serves both to reinforce conventional morality, and to 'remind' the woman reader of what she should value most. It also exemplifies the way in which gender ideology is constructed in terms of class concepts. Isabel's suffering, like her sinning, is the product of a class-specific version of sensitively refined femininity. The passage quoted above continues thus:

> It is possible remorse does not come to all erring wives so immediately as it came to Lady Isabel Carlyle – you need not be reminded that we speak of women in the higher positions of life. Lady Isabel was endowed with sensitively refined delicacy, with an innate, lively consciousness of right and wrong: a nature such as hers, is one of the last that may be expected to err; and, but for that most fatal misapprehension regarding her husband . . . she would never have forgotten herself. (*EL* 289–90)

This version of genteel femininity is what makes Isabel both a fallen-woman-as-victim and a heroine (albeit a dead one). The lower-class Affy Hallijohn, who has also been seduced and betrayed by Isabel's seducer, lacks this upper-class refinement and moral scrupulosity, and is, as a consequence, a ridiculed figure rather than a figure of pathos; her fall is associated with her social ambition as well as her sexual and social vulnerability. Between the upper-class victim and the lower-class hardened case stands Barbara Hare, the exemplification of the 'true womanhood' of the bourgeois ideal: a figure to be admired, but one who does not attract the emotional investment which the reader makes in Isabel.

East Lynne is not simply a warning to wives about the dangers of succumbing to delicious feelings for dashing young men; nor is it merely a nightmare vision of the maternal deprivation that will be visited on the mother who strays from her wifely duties. It is also a warning to women against succumbing to certain versions of femininity. If Braddon's two bestsellers dramatize the dangers of a manipulative, assertive woman (masquerading as the childlike feminine ideal) and the inadvertently criminal escapades of a boisterous 'Girl of the Period', Wood's apparently more conventional novel shows the dangers of conforming to the feminine ideal. Isabel Vane is precisely the passive, dependent, refined, innocent, childlike woman of the domestic, feminine ideal. It is these characteristics that make her simultaneously and paradoxically both a victim and a villainess. The reader who sees this paradox will see that there are questions to be asked about this ideal, and about the constraints that govern women's lives. There is more than one way to read even the conservative sensation novel.

A different form of maternal melodrama is found in *St Martin's Eve*, the novel in which Wood makes her contribution to the sensation novel's collection of madwomen. If *East Lynne* represents the introverted form of the over-invested mother in Isabel Vane, whose maternal excess is masochistically turned in on herself, then Charlotte Norris (later St John) in *St Martin's Eve* represents maternal excess in demonic, extroverted form. Charlotte has inherited her father's madness, but this hereditary taint only becomes apparent following the birth of her son, whom she loves to distraction, and to the exclusion of her husband.

> The frail little infant . . . had become to her the greatest treasure earth ever gave her; her love for him was of that wild, impassioned, all-absorbing nature, known, it is hoped, but to few, for it never visits a well-regulated heart. (pp. 39–40)

Charlotte's maternal excess is directed against her husband's heir, the son of his first marriage. Her mad, jealous rages against him culminate in a physical attack like Lady Audley's attack on Robert Audley, and the heir perishes in a fire. It is hardly to be supposed that the demonic mother should be allowed to get away with this process of unnatural selection; her own son dies (of consumption inherited from his father), and she is incarcerated in an asylum.

Even when it is represented in this demonic form, maternal excess and its sufferings contain a weight of sympathy which contradicts the overt moral message of the text. Like Magdalen Vanstone's quasi-criminal scheming, Charlotte's madness can also be viewed (and it is at points experienced in this way) as the understandable rage of the woman who is disempowered by her economic dependency, and by a legal system which does not recognize her claims or those of her child. On the other hand, this particular representation of the demonic mother offers a nightmare vision of what women were taught to fear that they might become if they did not submit to the regulation of their passions.

Like *East Lynne* and *St Martin's Eve*, most of Wood's other novels of the sensation decade are also stories of the control and containment of desire circulating within the family. Like most sensation novels, Wood's narratives represent this process in terms of rivalries within or between families, and between different generations and different social classes. Complicated inheritance plots (often involving lost or altered wills) and irregular or clandestine marriages play an important part in articulating this process. Most of Wood's plots involve a transfer of social power and moral authority from an effete, over-refined or decadent aristocracy (or those who ape aristocratic codes and practices) to the more robust representatives of the yeomanry or bourgeoisie, who are invested with the bourgeois virtues of thrift, hard work and strict conscience.

The moral scrupulosity of the strict conscience, the titillating spectacle of a man and woman of 'refined delicacy thrust by circumstances into extremely indelicate situations',[33] is one of the main sources of sensationalism in Wood's novels. Many critics attribute the sense of moral and social strain that attends Wood's preoccupation with delicate characters in indelicate situations to her own social insecurities as the daughter of a provincial glove manufacturer and the wife of a minor shipping agent who was pensioned off on account of his mental instability. This may well be the case, but this strain is also an integral part of a moral discourse which is constructed along class lines. The 'strained sufferings', arising from the 'entirely artificial predicaments' and 'exaggerated notions of honour'[34] of Wood's characters, articulate the tortuous (and tortured) process by which socially constructed, gendered subjectivities are produced.

In her dramas of moral scrupulosity, Wood brings together the conventions of popular melodrama and sentimental domestic fiction. The result is neither a mixing together of the two forms nor an assimilation of the one by the other. Instead, the two forms exist in what Bakhtin[35] describes as a dialogic relation. In many of Wood's novels (and certainly in *East Lynne*) this dialogue is a destabilizing process, in which the (originally) lower-class form of melodrama subverts the forms and norms of the middle-class sentimental novel.

4

The Sensation Legacy

Just as the phenomenon of sensationalism existed before the term entered general usage, sensation conventions and plots continued their existence long after the term went out of fashion. Patrick Brantlinger has suggested that the heirs of the sensation novel are the popular genres of the twentieth century – 'modern mystery, detective and suspense fiction and films'.[1] In this concluding section I want to argue that the impact of sensationalism on nineteenth-century fiction (and hence on fiction in general) was much more profound and enduring than Brantlinger's model would allow. The tentacles of sensationalism spread widely and deeply into many different kinds of fiction in the mid-Victorian period, and stretched out their reach as far as Hardy and his contemporaries at the end of the century.

In talking about the legacy of sensation fiction I want to avoid the idea of 'influence'. Throughout this study I have tried to argue that the sensation phenomenon in general and the individual novels I have been discussing were produced by and were engagements with a specific literary and historical moment. Those novels of the nineteenth century which have more readily found their way into 'great traditions' and onto literary syllabuses were part of the same literary-historical formation as the sensation novel. All novelists of the 1850s, 1860s (and beyond), whether or not they were labelled as sensationalists, worked with complex multiple plots, and engaged in the process of defining, reworking and redefining realism. However extreme their plots and their rhetoric, sensation novels were concerned with many of the same issues as the so-called mainstream Victorian novel: class, sex, money, family, morals, manners, marriage and social change. Similarly, sensation types, sensation plots and sensation machinery were integral parts of the storehouse of conventions upon which all Victorian novelists drew.

The sensation novel's appropriation and revision of melodrama was a project undertaken by numerous other nineteenth-century writers, from Charles Dickens to Thomas Hardy. Many contemporary critics regarded Dickens as the founder of the 'sensation school'. Certainly, right from the beginning of his career Dickens had anticipated the sensationalists' interest in crime and criminals. Several of Dickens's novels from the 1840s and 1850s also anticipated the sensation novel's concern with women with a secret and with problematic marriages; *Dombey and Son* (1846) and *Bleak House* (1852) are two of the most obvious examples. In the latter novel, Dickens also made use of the detective as the hunter out of the secrets of women, the secrets of the family and the evils of society. *Great Expectations*, which was reviewed alongside *The Woman in White*, has many sensation elements, including numerous criminals and men and women with dark secrets; like many sensation novels it contrives to suggest that respectable society conceals and is supported by a dark, criminal underlife. Like Collins, Braddon and Wood, Dickens is what Peter Brooks calls a 'social melodramatist'.[2] His is a serious reworking of the forms of melodrama, which strives 'to articulate, to demonstrate, to "prove" the existence of a moral universe which, though put into question, masked by villainy and perversions of judgement, does exist'.[3]

If Dickens was a serious sensationalist, Anthony Trollope was one of the many novelists who parodied the excesses of the genre. *The Eustace Diamonds* parodically rewrites *The Moonstone* by constructing a plot around a vulgar, socially ambitious young woman who steals her own diamonds, as Cuff had erroneously suspected Collins's Rachel Verinder of doing. Elsewhere, however, Trollope occupies the terrain of sensation fiction on its own terms. *Orley Farm*, for example, centres on the familiar sensation situations of the lady of high social rank and moral reputation who has a dark secret in her past, and the complications arising from confusions over wills and codicils. The basic sensation ingredients of crime, violence and sexual scandal regularly formed part of the social and political novels of this writer, who thought that a good novel should be 'at the same time realistic and sensational'.[4]

George Eliot, who attacked the silly novels by lady novelists of the generation before she began writing, nevertheless made much use of the conventions of those silly lady novelists whose heyday coincided with the early years of her own career as a novelist. Eliot often had recourse to sensation effects and sensation machinery in her attempts to render the moral universe legible, and to develop a form of realism in which she could conduct her 'experiments in life', her 'endeavour to see what our thought and emotion may be capable of'.[5]

Felix Holt the Radical, published in the middle of the sensation decade (1866), bears many of the hallmarks of the sensation novel. At the centre of the plot is Mrs Transome, an imperious woman with a taste for 'dangerous French authors', who radiates repressed passion and 'bitter discontent'. She is also a woman with a secret, which involves an adulterous affair and its continuing results. Mrs Transome's secret functions in the same way as the secrets of the sensation novels: a cross-class, illicit, sexual liaison undermines the upper classes, puts them in the power of their social inferiors, and disrupts the stability and continuity of the family and its property. The similarities between George Eliot and her sensational sisters did not go unremarked. The *Contemporary Review* described 'Lady Audley and Mrs Transome . . . [as] true twin sisters of fiction', and accused Eliot of joining hands with Braddon in reversing 'the grand old idea of . . . heroic behaviour, by cunningly eliciting our sympathy for individuals placed in doubtful circumstances, who fall into falsely tragical positions because of their weakness'.[6]

Even *Middlemarch*, the archetypal novel of high Victorian realism and moral seriousness, is not without sensation elements. The Dorothea, Casaubon, Ladislaw triangle (a sort of shadow bigamy plot) could have come straight from the sensation novel, as could the relationship of Rosamund with Lydgate and Ladislaw. The seemingly respectable banker, Bulstrode, has the obligatory secret skeleton in his past, and Raffles turns up as if from a sensation novel to provide the necessary plot machinery to expose it. Eliot's final novel, *Daniel Deronda*, also has many sensational features, as Barbara Hardy has noted: 'tangled and intricate intrigue', 'lost fathers and unknown mothers', 'melodramatic confrontations', 'mysterious past passions', illegitimate children and other 'skeletons in cupboards'.[7] It also has (like *The Moonstone*) the not-quite-wife and family in the villa who, in this case, emerge from their concealment to confront the heroine with an unpleasant truth about the man she is about to marry. But the most remarkable aspect of the sensationalism of this novel is its development of 'the actual psychology of sensation', its dramatization of Gwendolen's irrational fears and its exploration of her 'nervous equipment'.[8] Gwendolen's moral character is articulated in terms of her nervous sensations (which the reader is also made to feel), and her moral development begins in sensations of fear and terror.

Thomas Hardy's first novel, *Desperate Remedies* (published anonymously in 1871), was an example of sensationalism run riot. It was, as Hardy wrote in his Preface, a 'long and intricately inwrought chain of circumstance' involving 'murder, blackmail, illegitimacy, impersonation, eavesdropping, multiple secrets, a suggestion of bigamy, amateur and professional detectives'.[9] Although Hardy was later to disown the sensationalism of his early work as quite against his natural grain, sensational and melodramatic concerns and modes of representation continued to be an important part of his fiction. They are evident in the rhetorical excess of his style, particularly in his representation of female characters: the Braddonesque 'Queen of the Night' passage on Eustacia Vye (*The Return of the Native*) and the anatomizing of Tess Durbeyfield come to mind. Sensationalism is also present in Hardy's reliance on coincidence, and in the way in which his plots are shaped by the secrets of the past habitually returning to mould the present and future lives of his characters. Hardy's sensational antecedents can also be seen in his treatment of the 'deadly war waged between flesh and spirit',[10] and his persistent focus on troubled marriages and the problematic nature of the institution of marriage.

Hardy's representation of a deterministic Darwinian universe in which the characteristic experiences are suffering, anxiety and frustrated aims continues that revision of the conventions and moral vision of popular melodrama which was begun by the sensation novelists of the 1860s. For the sensationalists, as for several of the other novelists discussed in this section, and especially for Hardy, the abstract struggle between moral absolutes which was staged in the popular melodrama became a much more historically and socially particularized set of struggles. These were played out in a fragmented world in which the boundaries between moral categories were increasingly blurred and relativized. In the sensation fiction of the sixties the happy ending of marriage and an integrated social life and/or the final triumph of bourgeois virtue remained a possibility. It was regularly pulled out of the top hat in order to reassure readers whose moral universe and social convictions other aspects of the sensation plot so effectively disturbed. The resolution of the sensation plot is often achieved against the grain of both the narrative and moral puzzles of which it is constructed, and readers are left with the uneasy feeling that the supposedly civilized social surfaces of the age of materialism and progress are neither as civilized nor as natural as they were supposed to be.

Notes

CHAPTER 1. THE SENSATION PHENOMENON

1. 'Sensation Novels', *Quarterly Review*, 133 (1863), 512.
2. 'What is sensational about the sensation novel?', *Nineteenth Century Fiction*, 37 (1982), 1.
3. Ibid., 4.
4. P. D. Edwards, *Some Mid-Victorian Thrillers: The Sensation Novel, Its Friends and Foes* (St Lucia, Queensland, 1971), 4.
5. T. Richards, *The Commodity Culture of Victorian England: Advertising and Spectacle, 1851-1914* (London, 1991), 55.
6. J. B. Taylor, *In the Secret Theatre of Home: Wilkie Collins, Sensation Narrative and Nineteenth-Century Psychology* (London, 1988).
7. 'The Queen's English', *Edinburgh Review*, 120 (1864), 53.
8. Quoted in K. Tillotson, Introduction to Wilkie Collins, *The Woman in White* (Boston, 1969), p. xiii.
9. Edwards, 4.
10. Quoted in W. Hughes, *The Maniac in the Cellar: the Sensation Novel of the 1860s* (Princeton, NJ, 1980), 18.
11. N. Page, *Wilkie Collins: The Critical Heritage* (London, 1974), 169.
12. 'Belles Lettres', *Westminster Review*, 20 (1866), 269.
13. H. L. Mansel, 'Sensation Novels', *Quarterly Review*, 133 (1863), 482-3.
14. H. James, 'Miss Braddon', *The Nation*, 9 November 1865, p. 594.
15. Ibid., 594.
16. M. Oliphant, 'Novels', *Blackwood's*, 102 (1867), 209.
17. T. Todorov, *Mikhail Bakhtin: The Dialogical Principle*, trans. W. Godzich (London, 1984), 80.
18. F. Jameson, *The Political Unconscious: Narrative as a Socially Symbolic Act* (London, 1981), 141.
19. Mansel, 486.
20. M. Oliphant, 'Sensation Novels', *Blackwood's*, 91 (1862), 569.
21. Mansel, 484.
22. Ibid., 485.
23. Ibid., 483.

24. B. Kalikoff, *Murder and Moral Decay in Victorian Popular Literature* (Ann Arbor, Mich., 1986).
25. W. F. Rae, 'Sensation novelists: Miss Braddon', *North British Review*, 43 (1965), 204.
26. L. Pykett, *The Improper Feminine: The Women's Sensation Novel and the New Woman Writing* (London, 1992).
27. Kalikoff, 97.
28. P. Brooks, *The Melodramatic Imagination* (New Haven, Conn., 1976).
29. M. Vicinus, ' "Helpless and Unfriended": nineteenth-century domestic melodrama', *New Literary History*, 13 (1981), 128.
30. Brooks, 11–12.
31. Mansel, 485.
32. R. Williams, *The Long Revolution* (London, 1965), 67.

CHAPTER 2. WILKIE COLLINS: QUESTIONS OF IDENTITY

1. Hughes, 138.
2. See J. B. Taylor, *In the Secret Theatre of Home* (London, 1988), and E. Showalter, *The Female Malady* (London, 1987).
3. Showalter, *The Female Malady*.
4. Hughes, 159.
5. Page, 143.
6. W. Benjamin, *Charles Baudelaire: A Lyric Poet in the Era of High Capitalism* (London, 1973), 40.
7. See *The Political Unconscious*
8. P. Brantlinger, 'What is sensational about the sensation novel?', *Nineteenth Century Fiction* (1982), 14.
9. R. Williams, *The English Novel from Dickens to Lawrence* (London, 1985), 16.

CHAPTER 3. THE WOMEN'S SENSATION NOVEL

1. E. S. Dallas, 'Lady Audley's Secret', *The Times*, 18 November 1862, 8.
2. M. Oliphant, 'Novels', *Blackwood's*, 102 (1867), 274–5.
3. Quoted in R. L. Woolf, *Sensational Victorian: The Life and Fiction of Mary Elizabeth Braddon* (New York, 1979), 193.
4. J. Tomkins, *Sensational Designs: The Cultural Work of American Fiction, 1790–1816* (Oxford, 1985), 123.
5. T. Modleski, *Loving with a Vengeance: Mass-produced Fantasies for Women* (London, 1984), 25.
6. Ibid., 20.
7. J. Radway, *Reading the romance: Women, Patriarchy and Popular Literature* (London, 1987).

8. 'Writing fictions: femininity in the 1950s', in J. Radford, *The Progress of Romance: The Politics of Popular Fiction* (London, 1986).
9. *The Alienated Reader: Women and Popular Romantic Literature in the Twentieth Century* (London, 1991).
10. C. Gledhill (ed.), 'Pleasurable Negotiations', in E. D. Pribram, *Female Spectators: Looking at Film and Television* (London, 1988), 66.
11. J. McCarthy, 'Novels with a purpose', *Westminster Review*, 82 (1864), 47.
12. *Athenaeum*, 3 December 1864, 743.
13. Ibid., 743–4.
14. J. Fahnestock, 'Bigamy: the rise and fall of a convention', *Nineteenth Century Fiction*, 36 (1981), 65.
15. M. Oliphant, 'Novels', Blackwood's, 102 (1867), 268.
16. Ibid., 259.
17. E. Showalter, 'Family secrets and domestic subversion: rebellion in the novels of the eighteen-sixties', in A. Wohl, *The Victorian Family: Structure and Stresses* (London, 1978), 104.
18. *North British Review*, 43 (1865), 203.
19. S. Shuttleworth, 'Demonic Mothers: Ideologies of bourgeois motherhood in the mid-Victorian era', in L. Shires, *Rewriting the Victorians* (London, 1992), 32.
20. Oliphant, 'Novels', *Blackwood's*, 102 (1867), 260.
21. 'Miss Braddon', *The Nation*, 9 November 1865, 593.
22. Quoted in Woolf, 126.
23. W. F. Rae, 'Sensation novelists: Miss Braddon', *North British Review*, 43 (1865), 187.
24. Ibid., 186.
25. Quoted in Woolf, 137.
26. *The Improper Feminine*.
27. Hughes, 111.
28. Ibid., 155.
29. See N. Armstrong, *Desire and Domestic Fiction* (New York, 1987), and Shuttleworth, 'Demonic Mothers'.
30. S. S. Ellis, *The Mothers of England, their influence and responsibility* (London, 1843), 253.
31. W. Acton, *The Functions and Disorders of the Reproductive Organs in Childhood, In Youth, In Adult Age, and in Advanced Life considered in their Physiological, Social and Psychological Relations* (London, 1862), 102–3.
32. L. Williams, ' "Something else besides a mother": *Stella Dallas* and the maternal melodrama', in C. Gledhill, *Home is Where the Heart is* (London, 1987), 305.
33. Hughes, 117.
34. Ibid., 118.

35. M. Bakhtin, *Problems of Dostoevsky's Poetics* (Minneapolis, Minn., 1963) and *The Dialogic Imagination* (Austin, Tex., 1981).

CHAPTER 4. THE SENSATION LEGACY

1. Brantlinger, 1.
2. Brooks, 22.
3. Ibid., 20.
4. *Autobiography* (London, 1950), 227.
5. G. Haight, *The George Eliot Letters*, vol. VI (London, 1956), 216.
6. H. A. Page, 'The Morality of Literary Art', *Contemporary Review*, 5 (1867), 179.
7. Introduction to *Daniel Deronda*, (Harmondsworth, 1962), 27.
8. Ibid.
9. Hughes, 173.
10. Preface to *Jude the Obscure* (Harmondsworth, 1985), 39.

Select Bibliography

The date given after the place of publication is the date of the edition to which I have referred. When I have not used the first edition, and when the information is important, I have also included the date of first publication.

SENSATION NOVELS OF THE 1860s

Works by Mary Elizabeth Braddon
Aurora Floyd (1863; London, 1984).
The Doctor's Wife (London, 1864).
Eleanor's Victory (London, 1863).
Henry Dunbar (1864; London: Maxwell, n.d.).
John Marchmont's Legacy (London, 1863).
Lady Audley's Secret (1862; Oxford, 1987).
Run To Earth (London, 1868).

Works by Rhoda Broughton
Cometh Up as a Flower (1867; London, 1898).
Not Wisely But Too Well (1867; London, 1967).

Works by William Wilkie Collins
Armadale (1864–6; Oxford, 1989).
The Moonstone (1868; Harmondsworth, 1986).
No Name (1862; Oxford, 1986).
The Woman in White (1860; Oxford, 1980).

Works by Ellen Wood
East Lynne (1861; London, 1984).
Lord Oakburn's Daughters (1864; London, 1895).
St Martin's Eve (1866; London, 1905).
Trevlyn Hold (1864; London, 1886).
Verner's Pride (1863; London, 1893).

BIOGRAPHICAL AND CRITICAL STUDIES

'Belles Lettres', *Westminster Review*, 20 (1866), 269–70.

Brantlinger, P., 'What is sensational about the sensation novel?', *Nineteenth Century Fiction*, 37 (1982), 1–28.

Clarke, W., *The Secret Life of Wilkie Collins* (London, 1988).

Collins, W. W., *My Miscellanies* (London, 1983).

Dallas, E. S., 'Lady Audley's Secret', *The Times*, 18 November 1862, 8.

Edwards, P. D., *Some Mid-Victorian Thrillers: The Sensation Novel, Its Friends and Foes* (St Lucia, Queensland, 1971).

Fahnestock, J., 'Bigamy: the rise and fall of a convention', *Nineteenth Century Fiction*, 36 (1981), 47–71.

Hughes, W., *The Maniac in the Cellar: the Sensation Novel of the 1860s* (Princeton, NJ, 1980).

James, H., 'Miss Braddon', *The Nation*, 9 November 1865, 593–5. Reprinted in *Notes and Reviews* (Cambridge, Mass., 1981), 108–16.

Jewsbury, G., review of J. B. Harwood's *Lord Lynn's Wife*, *Athenaeum*, 3 December 1864, 743–4.

Kaplan, E. A., 'The Political Unconscious in the maternal melodram: Ellen Wood's *East Lynne*', in D. Longhurst, *Gender, Genre and Narrative Pleasure* (London, 1989).

Loesberg, J., The ideology of narrative form in sensation fiction', *Representations*, 13 (1986), 115–38.

McCarthy, J., 'Novels with a purpose', *Westminster Review*, 82 (1864), 24–49.

Mansel, H. L., 'Sensation Novels', *Quarterly Review*, 133 (1863), 481–514.

Michell, S., 'Sentiment and suffering: women's recreational reading in the 1860s', *Victorian Studies*, 21 (1977), 29–45.

Oliphant, M., 'Novels', *Blackwood's*, 94 (1863), 168–83.

—'Novels', *Blackwood's*, 102 (1867), 257–80.

—'Sensation Novels', *Blackwood's*, 91 (1862), 464–84.

O'Neil, P., *Wilkie Collins* (London, 1988).

'Our Female sensation Novelists', *Christian Remembrancer*, 46 (1863), 209–36.

Page, N., *Wilkie Collins: The Critical Heritage* (London, 1974).

'The Queen's English', *Edinburgh Review*, 120 (1864), 37–57.

Rae, W. F., 'Sensation novelists: Miss Braddon', *North British Review*, 43 (1865), 180–204.

Rance, N., *Wilkie Collins and Other Sensation Novelists* (London, 1991).

Showalter, E., 'Family secrets and domestic subversion: rebellion in the novels of the eighteen-sixties', in A. Wohl, *The Victorian Faniliy: Structure and Stresses* (London, 1978).

Shuttleworth, S., 'Demonic Mothers: Ideologies of bourgeois motherhood in the mid-Victorian era', in L. Shires, *Rewriting the Victorians* (London, 1992).

Taylor, J. B., *In the Secret Theatre of Home: Wilkie Collins, Sensation Narrative and Nineteenth-Century Psychology* (London, 1988).

Tillotson, K., 'The lighter reading of the eighteen-sixties', introduction to Wilkie Collins, *The Woman in White* (Boston, Mass., 1969).

Vicinus, M., ' "Helpless and Unfriended": nineteenth-century domestic melodrama', *New Literary History*, 13 (1981), 127–43.

Woolf, R. L., *Sensational Victorian: The Life and Fiction of Mary Elizabeth Braddon* (New York, 1979).

BACKGROUND READING

Acton, W., *The Functions and Disorders of the Reproductive Organs in Childhood, In Youth, In Adult Age, and in Advanced Life Considered in their Physiological, Social and Psychological Relations* (1857; London, 1862).

Armstrong, N., *Desire and Domestic Fiction* (New York, 1987).

Austin, A., 'The Poetry of the Period: Mr Swinburne', *Temple Bar* 26 (1869), 457–74.

Bakhtin, M., *The Dialogic Imagination*, trans. C. Emerson and M. Holquist (Austin, Tex., 1981).

—*Problems of Dostoevsky's Poetics*, ed. and trans. C. Emerson (Minneapolis, Minn., 1963).

Benjamin, W., *Charles Baudelaire: A Lyric Poet in the Era of High Capitalism* (London, 1973).

Booth, M., *Victorian Spectacular Theatre, 1850–1910* (London, 1981).

Brooks, P., *The Melodramatic Imagination* (New Haven, Conn., 1976).

Cawaelti, J. G., *Mystery, Adventure and Romance* (Chicago, Ill., 1976).

Ellis, S. S., *The Mothers of England, their influence and responsibility* (London, 1843).

Fowler, B., *The Alienated Reader: Women and Popular Romantic Literature in the Twentieth Century* (London, 1991).

Gledhill, C., 'Pleasurable Negotiations', in E. D. Pribram, *Female Spectators: Looking at Film and Television* (London, 1988).

Gledhill, C. (ed.), *Home is Where the Heart is: Studies in Melodrama and the Woman's Film* (London, 1987). Has several useful essays on melodrama, maternal melodrama, the male gaze, feminine viewing positions, etc.

Haight, G., *The George Eliot Letters*, vol. VI (London, 1956).

Hardy, B., Introduction to George Eliot, *Daniel Deronda* (Harmondsworth, 1962).

Hardy, T., *Jude the Obscure* (1894; Harmondsworth, 1985).

Helsinger, E. K., *et al.* (eds), *The Woman Question: Society and Literature in Britain and America, 1837–1883*, 3 vols. (Manchester, 1983). Volume 3 is particularly useful for the study of the sensation novel.

Holcombe, L., 'Victorian wives and property: reform of the married woman's property law, 1857–1882', in M. Vicinus, *A Widening Sphere: Changing Roles of Victorian Women* (London, 1980).

Jameson, F., *The Political Unconscious: Narrative as a Socially Symbolic Act* (London, 1981).

Kalikoff, B., *Murder and Moral Decay in Victorian Popular Literature* (Ann Arbor, Mich., 1986).

Light, A., 'Writing fictions: femininity in the 1950s', in J. Radford, *The Progress of Romance: The Politics of Popular Fiction* (London, 1986).

Linton, E. L., 'The Girl of the Period', *Saturday Review*, 14 March 1868, 339–40.

Mill, J. S. *The Subjection of Women* (London, 1869).

Modleski, T., *Loving with a Vengeance: Mass-produced Fantasies for Women* (London, 1984).

Page, H. A. (A. H. Japp), 'The Morality of Literary Art', *Contemporary Review*, 5 (1867), 161–89.

Palmer, J., *Potboilers: Methods, Concepts and Case Studies in Popular Fiction* (London, 1991).

Poovey, M., *Uneven Developments: The Ideological Work of Gender in Mid-Victorian England* (London, 1989).

Pykett, L., *The Improper Feminine: The Women's Sensation Novel and the New Woman Writing* (London, 1992).

Radway, J., *Reading the romance: Women, Patriarchy and Popular Literature* (London, 1987).

Richards, T., *The Commodity Culture of Victorian England: Advertising and Spectacle, 1851–1914* (London, 1991).

Showalter, E., *The Female Malady* (London, 1987).

—*A Literature of Their Own* (London, 1978).

Todorov, T., *Mikhail Bakhtin: The Dialogical Principle*, trans. W. Godzich (London, 1984).

Tomkins, J., *Sensational Designs: The Cultural Work of American Fiction, 1790–1816* (Oxford, 1985).

Trodd, A., *Domestic Crime and the Victorian Novel* (London, 1989).

Trollope, A., *Autobiography* (1883; London 1950).

Walbank, A., *Queens of the Circulating Library* (London, 1950).

Williams, L., ' "Something else besides a mother": *Stella Dallas* and the maternal melodrama', in C. Gledhill, *Home is Where the Heart is* (London, 1987).

Williams, R., *The English Novel from Dickens to Lawrence* (London, 1985).

—*The Long Revolution* (London, 1965).

Index

New and Forthcoming Titles
in the New Series of
WRITERS AND THEIR WORK

PUBLISHED

Title	Author
John Clare	*John Lucas*
Joseph Conrad	*Cedric Watts*
John Donne	*Stevie Davies*
Doris Lessing	*Elizabeth Maslen*
Christopher Marlowe	*Thomas Healy*
Andrew Marvell	*Annabel Patterson*

IN PREPARATION

Title	Author
W.H. Auden	*Stan Smith*
Aphra Behn	*Sue Wiseman*
Angela Carter	*Lorna Sage*
Children's Literature	*Kimberley Reynolds*
Elizabeth Gaskell	*Kate Flint*
William Golding	*Kevin McCarron*
William Hazlitt	*J.B. Priestley; R.L. Brett (introduction by Michael Foot)*
George Herbert	*T.S. Eliot (introduction by Peter Porter)*
Henry James - The Later Novels	*Barbara Hardy*
James Joyce	*Steve Connor*
King Lear	*Terence Hawkes*
Sir Thomas Malory	*Catherine La Farge*
Ian McEwan	*Kiernan Ryan*
Walter Pater	*Laurel Brake*
Jean Rhys	*Helen Carr*
The Sensation Novel	*Lyn Pykett*
Edmund Spencer	*Colin Burrow*
J.R.R. Tolkien	*Charles Moseley*
Mary Wollstonecraft	*Jane Moore*
Virginia Woolf	*Laura Marcus*
William Wordsworth	*Jonathan Bate*

For a complete catalogue of new and forthcoming titles in WRITERS AND THEIR WORK - NEW SERIES and for a stocklist of the original series titles still available please contact:
The Publicity Department (WTW) Northcote House Publishers Ltd., Plymbridge House, Estover, Plymouth, Devon PL6 7PZ. United Kingdom. Tel: 0752 735251 / 695745 Fax: 0752 695699

PUBLISHED

DORIS LESSING
Elizabeth Maslen

Covering a wide range of Doris Lessing's works up to 1992, including all her novels and a selection of her short stories and non-fictional writing, this study demonstrates how Lessing's commitment to political and cultural issues and her explorations of inner space have remained unchanged throughout her career. Maslen also examines Lessing's writings in the context of the work of Bakhtin and Foucault, and of feminist theories.

Elizabeth Maslen is Senior Lecturer in English at Queen Mary and Westfield College, University of London.

0 7463 0705 5 paperback 80pp £5.99

JOSEPH CONRAD
Cedric Watts

This authoritative introduction to the range of Conrad's work draws out the distinctive thematic preoccupations and technical devices running through the main phases of the novelist's literary career. Watts explores Conrad's importance and influence as a moral, social and political commentator on his times and addresses recent controversial developments in the evaluation of this magisterial, vivid, complex and problematic author.

Cedric Watts, Professor of English at the University of Sussex, is recognized internationally as a leading authority on the life and works of Joseph Conrad.

0 7463 0737 3 paperback 80pp £5.99

JOHN DONNE
Stevie Davies

Raising a feminist challenge to the body of male criticism which congratulates Donne on the 'virility' of his writing, Dr Davies' stimulating and accessible introduction to the full range of the poet's work sets it in the wider cultural, religious and political context conditioning the mind of this turbulent and brilliant poet. Davies also explores the profound emotionalism of Donne's verse and offers close, sensitive readings of individual poems.

Stevie Davies is a literary critic and novelist who has written on a wide range of literature.

0 7463 0738 1 paperback 96pp £6.99

PUBLISHED

CHRISTOPHER MARLOWE
Thomas Healy

The first study for many years to explore the whole range of Marlowe's writing, this book uses recent ideas about the relation between literature and history, popular and élite culture, and the nature of Elizabethan theatre to reassess his significance. An ideal introduction to one of the most exciting and innovative of English writers, Thomas Healy's book provides fresh insights into all of Marlowe's important works.

Thomas Healy is Senior Lecturer in English at Birkbeck College, University of London.

0 7463 0707 1 paperback 96pp £6.99

ANDREW MARVELL
Annabel Patterson

This state-of-the art guide to one of the seventeenth century's most intriguing poets examines Marvell's complex personality and beliefs and provides a compelling new perspective on his work. Annabel Patterson – one of the leading Marvell scholars – provides comprehensive introductions to Marvell's different self-representations and places his most famous poems in their original context.

Annabel Patterson is Professor of English at Yale University and author of *Marvell and the Civic Crown* (1978).

0 7463 0715 2 paperback 96pp £6.99

JOHN CLARE
John Lucas

Setting out to recover Clare – whose work was demeaned and damaged by the forces of the literary establishment – as a great poet, John Lucas offers the reader the chance to see the life and work of John Clare, the 'peasant poet' from a new angle. His unique and detailed study portrays a knowing, articulate and radical poet and thinker writing as much out of a tradition of song as of poetry. This is a comprehensive and detailed account of the man and the artist which conveys a strong sense of the writer's social and historical context.

John Lucas has written many books on nineteenth- and twentieth-century literature, and is himself a talented poet. He is Professor of English at Loughborough University.

0 7463 0729 2 paperback 96pp £6.99

PUBLISHED

GEORGE HERBERT

T.S. Eliot

With a new introductory essay by **Peter Porter**

Another valuable reissue from the original series, this important study –
one of T. S. Eliot's last critical works – examines the writings of George
Herbert, considered by Eliot to be one of the loveliest and most profound
of English poets. The new essay by well-known poet and critic Peter
Porter reassesses Eliot's study, as well as providing a new perspective on
Herbert's work. Together, these critical analyses make an invaluable
contribution to the available literature on this major English poet.

0 7463 0746 2 paperback 80pp £5.99

FORTHCOMING

CHILDREN'S LITERATURE

Kimberley Reynolds

Children's literature has changed dramatically in the last hundred years
and this book identifies and analyses the dominant genres which have
evolved during this period. Drawing on a wide range of critical and
cultural theories, Kimberley Reynolds looks at children's private reading,
examines the relationship between the child reader and the adult writer,
and draws some interesting conclusions about children's literature as a
forum for shaping the next generation and as a safe place for developing
writers' private fantasies.

Kimberley Reynolds lectures in English and Women's Studies at
Roehampton Institute, where she also runs the Children's Literature
Research Unit.

0 7463 0728 4 paperback 96pp £6.99

FORTHCOMING

WILLIAM GOLDING

Kevin McCarron

This comprehensive study takes an interdisciplinary approach to the work of William Golding, placing particular emphasis on the anthropological perspective missing from most other texts on his writings. The book covers all his novels, questioning the status of *Lord of the Flies* as his most important work, and giving particular prominence to *The Inheritors, Pincher Martin, The Spire* and The Sea Trilogy. This in-depth evaluation provides many new insights into the works of one of the twentieth century's greatest writers.

Kevin McCarron is Lecturer in English at Roehampton Institute, where he teaches Modern English and American Literature. He has written widely on the work of William Golding.

0 7463 0735 7 paperback 80pp £5.99

WALTER PATER

Laurel Brake

This is the only critical study devoted to the works of Pater, an active participant in the nineteenth-century literary marketplace as an academic, journalist, critic, writer of short stories and novelist. Approaching Pater's writings from the perspective of cultural history, this book covers all his key works, both fiction and non-fiction.

Laurel Brake is Lecturer in Literature at Birkbeck College, University of London, and has written widely on Victorian literature and in particular on Pater.

0 7463 0716 0 paperback 96pp £6.99

ANGELA CARTER

Lorna Sage

Angela Carter was probable the most inventive British novelist of her generation. In this fascinating study, Lorna Sage argues that one of the reasons for Carter's enormous success is the extraordinary intelligence with which she read the cultural signs of our times – from structuralism and the study of folk tales in the 1960s – to, more recently, fairy stories and gender politics. The book explores the roots of Carter's originality and covers all her novels, as well as some short stories and non-fiction.

Lorna Sage teaches at the University of East Anglia, where she is currently Dean of the School of English and American Studies.

0 7463 0727 6 paperback 96pp £6.99

With ᴀᴇ Foot

This revised editic ᴇɪʀ WORK series now
includes three autl nd perceptive
nineteenth-century essayist and critic, William Hazlitt. In addition to the
classic works by J. B. Priestley and R. L. Brett, the book contains a
completely new study by Michael Foot - an acknowledged Hazlitt
commentator. Together , these three contributions provide an engaging
introduction to a writer whose original wit and acute observation of the
age in which he lived are as fascinating today as ever.

0 7463 0745 4 paperback c80pp £5.99

IAN McEWAN
Kiernan Ryan

This is the first book-length study of one of the most original and exciting
writers to have emerged in Britain in recent years. It provides an
introduction to the whole range of McEwan's work, examining his novels,
short stories and screenplays in depth and tracing his development from
the 'succès de scandale' of *First Love, Last Rites* to the haunting vision of
the acclaimed *Black Dogs*.

Kiernan Ryan is Fellow and Director of Studies in English at New Hall,
University of Cambridge.

0 7463 0742 X paperback c96pp £6.99